PUNISHMENT AND PRIVILEGE

SECOND EDITION

Edited by
Graeme R. Newman
Distinguished Professor Emeritus
University at Albany

HARROW AND HESTON
Publishers

NEW YORK & PHILADELPHIA

PUNISHMENT
AND
PRIVILEGE

SECOND EDITION

CONTENTS

1. Introduction to the second edition

Graeme R. Newman

The word "privilege" has become a darling of the discontented in recent years. It is a particularly useful word because it does not need any empirical data to prove whether or not the particular person or class of persons are privileged. The word itself is its evidence of "truth." It is of the same class of adjectives as "good" or "bad." It is a word that directly and inherently displays its own truth: a moral assertion that expresses the disdain or downright hatred of the person or class of persons to which it is applied. It matters not how such persons came to be privileged, or how they assert or use their privilege. Privileged persons therefore cannot prove that they are not privileged, no matter how much data they produce showing otherwise. Even if they produce evidence that they use their privilege wisely, humanely, justly, charitably, or for the good of personkind, no matter. They are privileged, and therefore, ultimately, they must be knocked from their pedestal and punished for their privilege.

Some of the papers in this volume are devoted to proving that the privileged, usually defined as rich people or corporations, gain advantage over the poor, in this case in the area of criminal punishment. It is important to note that there is a presumption in many of these papers that the rich gained their advantage by a kind of cheating, usually based on the idea that the poor are poor because they were exploited by the rich—in the early post-modern world, in which these papers were written, essentially reflecting neo-Marxist ideology. Putting the bible aside, the more recent disdain for the rich and the adoration of the heroic poor harks back to the enlightenment of the 18th century, such as Rousseau, Voltaire, and Montesquieu who blamed it all on the privilege of birth and inheritance, reflected in its most extreme form by the regal power of sovereigns of various kinds. The enlightenment thinkers should have known better, for they surely learned in their classical studies that the glorification of the poor at various times during the ancient Roman republic most likely led to civil war, followed by—the irony is painful—military dictatorships and finally several centuries of autocratic rule of Emperors, an autocratic rule that lived on after the Roman Empire was transformed into the Holy Roman Empire.

Today, however, papers proving that the privileged are privileged are no longer needed. It is taken as fact. And there is a very large amount of empirical evidence accumulated over the decades since this volume was put together, showing that the rich really are rich, live their lives with advantage, and that the poor really are poor, exploited daily by the rich who if they did not inherit their wealth, accumulated it from criminal or quasi criminal actions. That is, they took unfair advantage of the "system" whatever that may be: from the rich point of view, taking advantage of economic opportunities, just as Adam Smith advocated back in the 17th century. From the Marxist point of view, the only advantage available is to exploit the labor of the poor, who therefore remain poor. The poor are exploited because the system is rigged against them.

Wherever the truth lies in these mirror images of privilege and poverty, one thing is very clear from the papers in this volume when taken together: none of them criticize punishment itself (though there is a hint of this recognition shown by Braithwaite who suggests that punishment should only be used as a last resort). Whatever the purpose of punishment, whether retributive or deterrent, there is agreement, which continues even more strongly today considering the current mass incarceration binge in the Western world, that punishment is necessary. The criticisms that are made in the papers in this volume and papers even today on punishment, are not of punishment itself (usually incarceration of various sorts) but of its unequal distribution.

There is no suggestion at all (except by a few who want to replace it with love, but that is another story with its roots in Woodstock), that abolishing inequality would eradicate the need for punishment. Nor should there be, given the history of failed attempts to set up communal societies that endure. Where all people are equal, punishment remains because societies, even communes, must have their rules of engagement, if they are to function and survive, and rules are there for one thing and one thing only: to punish those who break them. One need only watch *Lord of the Flies* to understand that societies cannot survive without rules that spawn punishment (and a disinterested party to administer it), even though punishment itself brings with it many difficult problems. But to discuss these problems would take us beyond the scope of the present book. It is enough to understand that punishment occurs independently from the inequity of privilege. The rich will punish the poor and likewise, the poor, given the chance, will punish the rich (so much for the Romanovs, Louis XVI, Charles 1 and the rest). The fact is that to use punishment on another who has broken a rule is itself an act that reflects privilege: since punishment must be applied by one with the authority to do it, otherwise it is violence of one against another (Newman 2008). The question is, who has the authority to punish? And how did they get it?

A difficulty faced in a number of the papers, particularly that of Pontell et al., also addressed directly by Fisse, and the many papers written since, is what punishments are appropriate for "white collar" criminals (i.e., as noted earlier, corporations) who break the law? From the point of view of equity, the rich should be punished at least as much as the poor (or vice versa, the poor as little as the rich). How do you punish a corporation? Would it be reasonable to inflict the death penalty on a corporation? Would doing so be equivalent to inflicting the death penalty on an individual? How does one measure the total amount of punitive effects of a particular punishment? Would the death of a corporation, say, with a hundred employees who would lose their livelihoods, be more or less severe than the destruction of one life of a (lower class or poor) murderer? None of these questions has an answer. The problem is that the criminal law, at least in Western civilization since its inception, has been solely focused on the punishment of individuals. Perhaps this is because of the quasi-religious origins of Western criminal law (though this is doubtful since its roots are firmly rooted in Roman law which also was focused on individual criminality). Canon law fashioned itself on Roman law, reflecting the preoccupation of the guilt of individual criminals, developed to a sophisticated level during the Holy Inquisitions. It used the criminal law as an individualistic procedure of the finding of guilt and application of punishment of sinners—now called criminals. It was a logical step from the criminal law of the ancient Romans, which was motivated by two factors: personal animosity against the accused, but more often, a way of vilifying a political enemy. Offenders were not sinners, but political outcasts.

The obsession with catching criminals and convicting them takes up the largest part of viewing time of all TV shows everywhere. It is not surprising that all law enforcement bodies in the USA and their equivalents in most of the world—police, state troopers, military police, private police, the FBI, and perhaps now the CIA are single-mindedly devoted to catching, prosecuting, and convicting individual criminals. Whether TV emulates criminal justice or criminal justice emulates TV, is an open question. Though one particularly interesting fact is that there is (by comparison) little TV entertainment of the actual punishment of criminals, with some exceptions such as *OZ* and movies that depict the dramas of prison life, such as *Shawshank Redemption* though the latter mostly gain their traction by depicting the hero as wrongfully convicted. Crime dramas focus on the catching and interrogation (usually with some physical force or threat of violence, by a "rogue" police officer, e.g., Dirty Harry). The drama also unfolds as a cat and mouse game between the pursuing police officer or prosecutor and the cunning evil criminal. This obsession in real life policing, especially the FBI is so great that police agencies will actually commit crimes in order to entrap would-be criminals or "innocent" individuals into committing crimes. The FBI is renowned for this method, especially in the field of terrorism where they have a very poor record of catching actual terrorists and probably have caught and prosecuted most of their terrorists using entrapment techniques (Clarke and Newman 2006). And of course, their well-known use of the "perjury trap" works to convict suspects for lying to the FBI when they cannot find the evidence to convict them of actual criminal acts. The FBI has, in recent years, gone much further than this. They now use all the enforcement powers they have, which are considerable; late night break-ins and raids on suspects' houses to bring charges, threaten their families, reduce their suspects to poverty. This works very well against the "rich," which should make those on the left happy (well-known cases include the conviction of Martha Stuart for lying to the FBI and the destruction of the accounting firm Arthur Anderson and Associates, whose conviction was overturned unanimously by the Supreme Court, after the accused had spent a year in prison). There are other egregious cases as I will note further below.

The idea that there might be other measures that could be taken to reduce the opportunities to commit crime has barely touched the everyday practice of these law enforcement bodies. By this I do not mean deterrence, the forward-looking punishment, just-ified on the grounds that punishment will prevent future crimes (still not proven empirically, except in very prescribed circum-stances), and argued for persuasively (but incorrectly) in the van den Haag chapter. However, the research on situational crime prevention accumulated over the last several decades (Clarke 2016) shows that the re-arrangement of social and environmental circumstances that present opportunities for individuals to commit crime, can effectively prevent it. For example, one could arrest and punish individuals for car theft forever and never make a dent on the amount of car theft. Simply manufacturing cars that are designed to prevent theft (there is now a long history of the evolution of these techniques, see: Maxfield and Clarke 2004) manages to reduce crime and thus punishment. Situational crime prevention focusses on reducing opportunities for crime, does not target any class of individuals (rich or poor), has proven that crime can be reduced if not eliminated in specific areas, by designing crime prevention into products, services and places. (Clarke and Newman 2005). If this sounds far-fetched, and only applicable to street crime like car theft or shoplifting, there is much evidence that all kinds of crime, including fraud, cyber-crime, murder and terrorism, can be prevented using these techniques. Furthermore, if situational crime prevention were introduced into everyday policing, as the Center for Problem Oriented Policing (www.popcenter.org) advocates it would un-dercut the unshakeable belief of police that they can solve every problem by arresting someone—even though the empirical facts show that arresting people has little to do with reducing crime, except in very specific circumstances (Braga 2017). It has every-thing to do with punishing individuals, including the person at or during his arrest, as we have seen in recent well publicized cases. One case in particular where in 2014, Eric Garner died during his arrest by New York Police for selling contraband cigarettes in the street. For punishment to become a last resort as Braithwaite pleads, clearly the everyday operations of police must change radically. The arrest of individual suspects is the beginning of a painful process of punishment, not limited to the individual suspect, but also applied to his or her friends or family, taken to its extreme by the FBI, as we will see further below.

The move to regulate the criminogenic environment (social and physical) through situational prevention techniques (Freilich and Newman 2018) has arisen at the same time as the move to regulate citizen and corporate behavior through rules that are administered and overseen by various agencies, including the Federal Communications Commission, the Environmental Protection Agency, the Consumer Product Safety Commission the Food and Drug Administration, and a myriad of other agencies. Many of these agencies punish non-compliance as though they are crimes (though they are rarely called this). Since the publication of the first edition of this book, the rise of regulatory bodies has grown exponentially (Gurinskaya and Nalla (2018), to the point that one could well make the argument that the rich (corporations) are punished far more than are the poor, even to the extent of the death penalty for the corporations as happened with the Anderson case. We should note, though, as is the case with traditional crime and punishment (i.e. catching criminals and punishing them), the side-effects ("unintended consequences") of these regulatory, policing and punishing activities affect many, many others besides the targeted offender (whether corporate or individual), as recounted in the Fisse chapter. Unfortunately, the activities of most regulatory agencies themselves lack oversight, and their administrative procedures for enforcement of regulations do not demand the same burden of proof as does criminal law (in theory that is), nor is there a jury of peers, nor is there necessarily a judicial bench; more often than not, rules are administered by bureaucrats. There may or may not be right to appeal. It is not difficult to conclude that the essential motivation of many of these regulatory agencies is punishment, rather than prevention of harm. This applies especially when the FBI gets involved, as is clearly shown by the shocking case in which the CEO of a small medical device company was targeted by the FBI with the sole determination of getting a conviction regardless of whether there was a crime involved or not. If there was no crime, they would soon find one (Root and Saltarelli 2016)

So where is the privilege? As I write this introduction, the USA is in the midst of ballyhoo over spying by the FBI and other intelligence agencies on the Trump administration and campaign leading up to the presidential election in 2016. The FBI has performed, in the service of special counsel Mueller, in classic fashion: early morning break-ins and arrests, forcing acquaintances of the suspect to "flip" or "sing," using perjury traps and the rest. On the social and mainstream media, one theme prevails: that the perceived stratification of society between "the rich" and "the poor" has been transformed (perhaps temporarily) into "the establishment" or "deep state" depending on one's ideological leanings, and "the rest of us." If there are classes of persons, they are "the political class" and the "alienated class," the latter including both poor and not-so-poor. The political class, of course, is not poor, nor is it necessarily rich as in corporate rich, but it is certainly rich in its relationships with influential people, who are usually themselves rich, if not well connected with those who are. In other words the political class, no matter of what ideological pretention, depends on those with money for its expensive existence. Some of the alienated class may be poor, but my guess is that the poor have not noticed much of a difference. They are used to being ignored and called on only in times of political crisis. It is the rest, the very large majority who are alienated. Perhaps alienation is better than punishment. Though one suspects that, given the historical role that alienation has played in political movements of various kinds, retribution is always in the offing.

And speaking of retribution. All the contributors to this volume are/were white. It would be difficult to conceive of an edited book on punishment and privilege today that would not include a black author. Furthermore, the word "race" is mentioned but once in this entire volume. Nor do the words "African American, "blacks" or otherwise appear, though "non-white" does get a mention. Yet, the word "privilege" is most often today coupled with "white."

What is meant by "white privilege" is a question that demands a very complicated answer, taking us well beyond the bounds of this book. Historically, white civilization (that is Western civilization) appears to have spread its wings to cover large portions of planet earth. Its forebears, the Judeo-Christian, Greco-Roman law and ethic, created the industry, technologies and business acumen that made Western civilization and culture into what it is today. It made many people rich and it raised many people around the world out of poverty. Many also suffered along the way, and because of this, the West is vilified for its past, and perhaps still present, colonialism. It is the *ressentiment* against colonialism, despite its amazing achievements for the good, that simmers within such institutions as the United Nations—an institution created out of white privilege—supporting the frequent charges of racism, and demands for reparations for past misdeeds. How does the balance sheet of the good and the bad play out when the West is held to account?

Do facts matter here, when we try to assess the consequences, good and bad, of white privilege? If it is shown that blacks are punished more than whites (holding poverty constant or not) what is the solution? Replace those who punish with black punishers who are poor or not? These are mischievous questions, for which there are no easy answers, perhaps no answers at all. Punishment transcends class and race. This is because it is a universal necessity of social life, as Bernard in the final essay of this book, appears to conclude in his review of the great classical theorists (all white) of sociology. Without punishment, rules have no meaning; nor can punishment exist without rules to punish for. Punishment, to be just, must punish equally those who have broken rules; punish them for their actions, not for who they are.

2. Introduction to the first edition

W. Byron Groves and Graeme R. Newman

The first contribution to this volume (Jesilow, Pontell, and Geis) provides a fascinating and detailed analysis of the many variables which allow physicians to avoid punishment for Medicare and Medicaid fraud. Because misdeeds by physicians (e.g. overbilling) do not receive sufficient public or official attention, and because "professional" norms tend to insulate physicians from scrutiny by colleagues within the profession itself, many crimes committed by physicians are not taken seriously, or worse still, pass entirely unnoticed. In addition, Jesilow et al. point out that a beleaguered criminal justice system is hardly in a position to cope with crimes of this sort. Given the meager resources allocated for detecting crimes by physicians, their unfortunate conclusion is that the bulk of medical fraud is, and will continue to be, virtually impossible to detect. But the most ironic aspect of their discussion is that a not insignificant percentage of society's "healers" are promoting a criminogenic cancer of fraud and abuse which ultimately threatens to undermine public confidence in the Medicare/Medicaid program as a whole. As with so many authors in the area of white collar crime, Jesilow et al. conclude that so long as such crimes are not taken seriously, those committing them will continue to enjoy the fruits of their ill-gotten gains while avoiding the pains of punishment so often experienced by their less privileged counterparts.

The next article (Fisse) addresses an issue normally sidestepped in discussions of white-collar crime. That is: what can be done to effectively punish, deter, and/or rehabilitate white-collar and corporate offenders? After an exhaustive review of both the strengths and limitations of fines and monetary penalties, Fisse catalogues a number of options which might more effectively address crimes of the powerful. Some of these options include forcing corporate violators to distribute shares of stock to the state's crime victim compensation fund; insisting that corporations discipline themselves internally by means of corporate probation and punitive injunctions; mandating that corporations advertise their misdeeds so as to increase public awareness of corporate crimes; and finally, imposing community service functions on corporate violators as a means of achieving restitution for corporate misbehaviors. Each of these options is reviewed in great detail, and Fisse concludes that increased attention to these alternatives would make for much more efficient legal solution to a problem which is too often seen in economic (i.e., fines and monetary) terms. All told, Fisse's argument is comprehensive and convincing; it is the most constructive catalogue of reaction to white-collar crime available within a relatively short compass.

For those who enjoy paradoxes, the third article in this book (Braithwaite) is sure to capture your attention. The paradox is captured in what Braithwaite calls a theorem of justice, which states that where desert is greatest, punishment will be least. The argument, in brief, looks like this. on retributive grounds it is clear that white-collar and corporate criminals deserve more punishment than run-of-the-mill street criminals. After all business offenses cause much more objective harm than do common crimes: they are committed more frequently than common crimes, and public opinion surveys suggest that white collar criminals are perceived as more deserving of severe punishment than are common criminals. The rub, however, is that pursuing a policy of retributive punishment will do more harm than good for two reasons. First, corporations faced with the prospect of punitive sanctions will litigate cases endlessly in order to avoid punishment, and "justice delayed if profits retained." Second, to prevent greater harm in the future Braithwaite suggests that companies must be provided with incentives to report harmful activities (e.g., near misses due to culpable air traffic mismanagement). If companies were prosecuted for each and every instance of self-disclosure, incentives for self-disclosure would disappear, and with the ability to avoid potential disasters in the future. The competing values then, are protection of the public vs. just deserts, and the long and short of Braithwaite's position is that exclusive attention to justice would have disastrous consequences for public safety. What, then, is to be done? Can we accept a two-tiered justice system with just deserts for the poor and gentle persuasion for the rich? Clearly not, for this would entail "pandemic class injustice." In closing, Braithwaite plants the seeds for a meaningful solution to this dilemma by introducing his forthcoming theory of justice, which suggests that punishment be used as a mechanism of last resort, i.e., when there is no more constructive way of solving a social problem.

The fourth contribution to this volume (Groves and Frank) picks up where Braithwaite leaves off by suggesting that among those who commit crimes, punishment will be greatest where it is deserved the least. Relying on what they call a sociology of structured choice, the authors argue that the distribution of incentives and motivations throughout the class structure is such that lower class persons are more likely to commit (or, more accurately, more likely to choose to commit) those types of crime that are the most frequently and severely punished in our society. At the risk of oversimplifying their position, Groves and Frank argue that lower class persons are more determined to commit the types of crime that earn the most punishment, and that the coercions and temptations which beset lower class persons should be factored in when assessing both responsibility and the amount of punishment the impoverished defendant should receive. While other themes are discussed (e.g., the limitations of legal conceptions of responsibility as currently defined), the overarching issue is common to every article contained in this volume: how can the criminal justice system be manipulated such that we might achieve just results within the context of an unjust society?

The fifth contributor to this volume (Ernest van den Haag) provides us with yet another example of his seemingly endless capacity for making distinctions between the major rationales for punishment (e.g., retribution, deterrence, rehabilitation, and social defense). For those unfamiliar with these rationales, this article provides an excellent articulation of each position. For those acquainted with Professor van den Haag's views of punishment, the on-going shift from his earlier incorporation of a retributive rationale (his book *Punishing Criminals*) to a theory grounded in deterrence will be noteworthy. Among the many issues discussed are whether to punish more harshly for second and third offenses, whether preventive detention ("preemptive social defense") can be practically or morally justified, whether juveniles should be treated the same as adults, whether we need more prisons to deal effectively with the crime problem, whether rehabilitation is a worthy objective in sentencing, and whether parole should be abolished. As always, van den Haag defends his position on these issues with a fierce logic and an ever-present dedication to internal consistency.

But if it is consistency that we want, we will not find it in punishment. Van den Haag offers a challenging counterpoint to the writers of the previous chapters, for, while he virtually ignores the problem of privilege, he has become a strong advocate for punishment, especially deterrence. And isn't this where the previous writers actually end up? While Fisse still sees room for the retributive use of punishment, all writers in the chapters to this point speak as one in their advocacy of punishment as control; punishment as deterrence. They are aware of the difficulties with this position. Though they argue convincingly for a fairer distribution of punishment according to various egalitarian ideals, none of them has, in fact, given up punishment as such. While "regulation" or "control" seem to be the preferred alternatives it is also recognized (correctly) that deterrence is not in fact an effective method of controlling behavior—at least we have difficulty demonstrating this for conventional crime.

The only difference between them and van den Haag, then, is in their targets of control. While van den Haag seems satisfied to confine his advocacy for deterrence and incapacitation to the conventional criminal (which means lower class criminal), Jesilow, Fisse, Braithwaite, Groves et al. argue for either more punishment of the rich and powerful, or less punishment for the weak, so as to balance the scales of justice.

A most unsettling observation arises from these chapters. They seem to imply that the amount of behavior that either deserves punishment or that should be controlled through some form of punishment is far greater than that which is currently subjected to criminal processing. We have been told this for some years about conventional crime since the inception of victimization studies. Now, with the force of argument from the researcher of white-collar crime, we are convinced that the dark figure of white-collar crime exists in vast proportions.

If this is indeed the case, it would follow, if there were a direct (or even indirect) relation between crime and punishment, that there would be much more punishment administered to white-collar criminals than there is at present. We know, however, from the studies reviewed by Killias in chapter 8 that there is probably no link between the amount of crime and the amount of punishment. That the two exist in modern society independently is a startling discovery, and so difficult to understand in the conventional language of punishment philosophy. The retributive position especially, both historically and logically, must have an offense in order to punish. The wonder is, that in a society in which there is such an enormous array of behavior that could be punished, that so little actually is.

The remaining articles in the volume examine this question from quite different perspectives. Killias shows that, while we may never know how much punishment there is in a particular society, we can certainly compare the amount and forms of punishment across societies and establish a rough idea of whether particular societies have higher—or much higher—levels of punishment than others. Furthermore, he argues with persuasive empirical support, that there appears to be a strong relationship between the political freedom of a country, especially in terms of the centralization of control, and the unequal distribution of income, and the amount of punishment. It is as we would expect. The more totalitarian, the more the punishment. The more unequal the income distribution, the more the punishment.

A small number of venerable theorists has tried to explain the interesting fluctuations in the amount and forms of punishment over time and according to culture and these are reviewed by Killias. Needless to say, there is little agreement on why punishment takes on the forms it does, or why it fluctuates. Bernard, in the final chapter tries to identify how some of the classic theorists reached the conclusions they did concerning the functions of punishment in society. Durkheim, Simmel, Marx—were there any points of agreement? Perhaps only that punishment is an inevitable product of the particular society in which we find ourselves.

Pepinsky doesn't agree. In chapter 8, he argues that punishment has had its day, and it's time that we put it behind us. He can find nothing good to say about it and is careful not to use other words that could be substituted for it: control, deter, rehabilitate, discipline. These words have no place in Pepinsky's scheme. Rather, he seeks to eradicate the essential structure that makes punishment possible (part of its standard definition, in fact): authority. While he dismisses punishment as a form of legitimized violence (which, according to its standard definition it is: the intentional infliction of pain or suffering normally considered unpleasant), he argues, along with Christ, that "those who would sit in judgment on others must feel 'vulnerable' to the accused."

The history of punishment thus becomes the history of authority. The challenge for the future is to begin in a modest way, to break down authority structures, to establish through small groups and communities, a new way of developing social relationships: those that do not depend on the infliction of violence or its lesser though more insidious siblings, discipline and control. Whether this is possible, we do not know. It does seem to hark back to the good old days of "mechanical solidarity."

We do agree with Pepinsky, though, that the more punishment is used no matter what its justification, it seems to produce as much or more suffering than the original offense for which it was invoked. It is truly amazing that, in a field where the use of violence and infliction of suffering is so vast as in criminal punishment, we should find ourselves wanting both to administer it to new populations, but to eradicate it at the same time. The reader is invited to entertain this contradiction, and enjoy the challenges to conventional thinking on criminal punishment and its relationship to fairness and justice, which are contained in this volume.

3. Physician immunity from prosecution and punishment for medical program fraud*

Paul Jesilow, Henry N. Pontell and Gilbert Geis

Two facts are unarguable about crimes and other violations by physicians of the regulations that control the practice of medicine under the Medicaid and Medicare programs. The first is that there are considerable physical and fiscal harms; the second is that few who break the laws are apprehended, prosecuted, or convicted. The reasons for this situation provide the core material of the present paper; in this regard it provides detailed and specific case study material on a subject often addressed in general terms in the literature on white-collar crime: why it is that the perpetrators of upper-class offenses so readily avoid the stipulated legal consequences of their actions (Ross, 1907; Sutherland, 1934; Geis, 1967; Katz, 1979; Hagan and Parker 1985).

The illegal behavior by physicians participating in the Medicare and Medicaid programs offers special advantages for analyzing the punishment of white-collar offenders. Most importantly, physicians allow for the study of individual versus group, or corporate behavior. Recent studies of white collar crime have tended to see individual behavior within the context of corporate enterprise. Organizations are viewed as amalgamates of inter changeable operating personnel who behave on the basis of institutionalize requirements (Ermann and Lundman, 1982). Within the camouflage of the organization the individual is usually protected from sanctioning. As Braithwaite has noted, "[N]either the political will nor the prosecutorial resource exist to prove beyond a reasonable doubt that complex activities of a large company constitute a crime" (1981-82:482). That the situation Braithwaite describes for corporations is also valid for physicians is what this paper seek to examine and clarify.

Data for this study were obtained from official reports and face-to-face interviews with American Medical Association

(AMA) officials and Medicaid/Medicare administrators and enforcement officials in four states and in Washington, D.C. who are responsible for the integrity of the program: These persons included health department officials and investigators, federal agents in the Office of Inspector General and the Health Care Financing Ac ministration of the U.S. Department of Health and Human Services, stat prosecutors who handle medical fraud cases, officials and investigators in special Medicaid Fraud Control Units, and officials of state-contracted companies ("carriers" or "fiscal intermediaries") who administer payments for the benefit program. Their remarks are cited as from "personal interviews.

Fraud in Medicare/Medicaid

Estimates of the loss to the Medicare and Medicaid programs due to fraud that were provided to us by enforcement officials generally ranged from between ten and twenty-five percent of the almost $100 billion dollars expended annually. But most agents believe that the majority of physicians are honest. One official commented:

> I'll have to admit because of what I've seen, I've become very jaded about the medical profession, and I have to periodically sort of talk to myself and say, 'Hey, this is only a very, very small minority of people doing this type of thing.' And I truly believe that. (Personal interview).

It is believed, however, that most physicians occasionally "nickel and dime" the programs, much as many persons will occasionally steal small things from employers or fiddle on taxes. Still, schemes resulting in losses in the tens of thousands of dollars are common. Certainly, there seems to be no dearth of malefactors to explain low apprehension and conviction rates. Nor is the harm of the behavior inconsequential. Unnecessary surgery can be likened to manslaughter and assault: It kills and maims (Lanza-Kaduce, 1980). If nothing else, medical fraud diverts funds from proper channels and, as a result, detracts from the health care of citizens.

Hidden victimization

Numerous authors have commented on the hidden nature of white-collar crime (Braithwaite, 1982; Katz, 1979; Pepinsky and Jesilow, 1985). The actual amount of law and rule-breaking by physicians participating in medical benefit programs—estimates aside—can only be a matter of conjecture. It is not possible to calculate offense rates from either reports of victimization or from sample population surveys. Victims of medical fraud rarely know that they have been bilked or that an injury was the consequence of unnecessary and unwarranted medical procedures. Nor is any citizen sample especially cognizant of medical malevolence. Were citizens aware, such matters would not be apt to prove of much moment. Bilking insurance companies carries much different emotional meaning that being personally bilked.

Investigators who know the system are amazed that any doctor's wrongdoing would surface. "[T]he fish that jump in the boat. These are the only ones we get," explained an investigator. Physicians who are "smart" according to enforcement agents will choose to victimize the programs by overutilization ordering unnecessary tests and procedures. Such behavior is unlikely to be discovered and, if it is, will be considered "abuse" rather than labeled as fraud. "I think if a guy is smart he'll go with the over-utilization because he isn't going to go to jail for it" (personal interview). Easily recognizable patterns of aberrant behavior are rare, as most offenders cloak their misdeeds by hiding their frauds in a seemingly normal practice of medicine. The hidden nature of the crime of intentional over-utilization effectively limits the possibility that such behavior will be detected and sanctioned.

Professional norms

Criminal activities of physicians can come to the attention of other doctors and be reported to authorities. Physicians some-times become aware of misdeeds of colleagues through their professional practice. The professional model holds, in part, that in interacting with one another, individuals are presumed to exercise direct control over one another's behavior (Freidson 1975:9). Such offenses, however, are unlikely to be reported.

In regard to the rather lax policing of the profession, consider Professional Standard Review Organizations (PSROs) local physician groups that determine whether services are medically necessary and rendered in accordance with professional standards. PSROs represent an attempt by the government to increase the likelihood that aberrant physicians will be identified and sanctioned. They were also created for quality control in general and to protect the Medicare and Medicaid programs without imposing external policing efforts on doctors. For PSROs to function as effective control institutions they had to overcome a number of pressures generated from the medical profession itself. First, they had to be willing to label the practice of fellow physicians as deviant. But research by Freidson (1975) showed that doctors were more likely to see aberrant behavior in normative terms. That is, they tended to excuse the behavior as something any doctor might do. An example of this phenomenon is found in the case of a San Francisco physician found guilty of Medicaid fraud who was reelected to a hospital board soon thereafter. An investigator involved in the case expressed her shock to those doing the electing. She was told, "Well, everyone knows that Medicaid pay so little" (personal interview). The physician's fraudulent behavior, rather than being censored by his colleagues, was considered as a rather normative response to Medicaid's reimbursement schedule.

A second influence of the medical profession that may restrict the usefulness of PSROs in reporting illegalities stems from the confidentiality of the doctor-patient relationship. Research has shown that breaches of this relationship receive the most severe sanctions from colleagues (Abbott, 1983 A high-ranking official's feelings about PSROs are illustrative:

> They took a look at the broad picture in the health community and attempted to tell the carrier this is right or this is wrong and they were part and parcel of the whole medical society's system of attempting to cleanse itself or to monitor what they were doing. The unfortunate part about the PSRO — some PSROs are really effective, but then again — those that were successful and effective got run out of town. The unsuccessful ones were the kingpins of the local AMA. I had severe problems with a couple of PSROs. They didn't even want to give me records. I say, wait a minute. We pay you. What the hell are you talking about you won't give me records. You're working for the federal government. All this was sacrosanct information, this information on patients. (Personal interview).

For PSROs to function as effective policing agents (and thus increase the certainty that illegal acts are uncovered and sanctioned) would require a flouting of professional norms and would, as the above quote suggests, result in an estrangement between the PSRO and the local medical community a situation that appears improbable. Indeed, the grand blueprint for ubiquitous national PSRO surveillance now has been abandoned in favor of optional recourse to them where it appears they might be of some use.

System capacity

Numerous authors have noted that the size of resources devoted to criminal justice defines limits to the sanctioning of offenders (Geerken and Gove, 1975; Blumstein et al., 1978; Pontell, 1984). The existing crime rate can overload the system. A beleaguered system generates less punishment in order to continue to sanction offenders (Pepinsky, 1980; Pontell, 1982). In addition, certainty of punishment declines as the system no longer is able to investigate, apprehend and process some reported as well as unreported crimes. The budget of enforcement agencies looms large as a limit to the sanctioning of white-collar crime as well (Katz, 1979). A high-ranking Medicare enforcement official noted in this regard that, "to go after these guys we need an army and all we've got is half a battalion, if that." Most individuals we interviewed felt that if they could investigate more crime, they would certainly find it. The current enforcement system, however, already is overloaded.

Intermediaries, who are contracted by the state and federal governments to pay health care providers for services rendered to Medicare and Medicaid patients, are normally insurance companies such as Blue Cross/Blue Shield. At the start of the programs it was felt that participation would be hampered if physicians had to submit bills to the government. Rather, it seemed appropriate to hire insurance companies already involved in payment activities to perform this task. According to their Medicare and Medicaid contracts, intermediaries have to do some utilization review of the bills submitted. Such control activities that do exist, however, are minimal. The companies have no fiscal incentive to scrutinize requests for payment. Most of their efforts concern making sure that forms are filled out correctly. In the early years of the programs, intermediaries totally ignored fraud and abuse Their government-supplied budgets compensated them only for paying the bills. There was no money allocated for ferreting out criminal and abusive behavior.

Skyrocketing health care costs combined with government hearings and media attention required that something be done about fraud and abuse in the mid-1970s. The federal government began to require the intermediaries to have at least one person assigned to fraud and abuse activities. The Reagan administration's budget cuts have hampered even these minima] efforts. A federal official explains:

Historically, there has been no specific line item in contracts or budgets devoted to program integrity activities. Whenever we have worked with contractors to try and get them to do something in the program integrity area, they have always had to use people for whom funds were budgeted someplace in their budget, but there was never any place for program integrity. Now it's even worse. For the current budgets they are told to fund mandatory items first, such as bill processing, and then if they have any money left after that they can do the non-mandatory things which get into medical review, utilization review, the areas that do work for program integrity... [Utilization review] ...isn't going to be done because they aren't going to voluntarily take money away from that part of their operation on which they are scored how good an intermediary or carrier they are has something to do with how quickly they process claims and how much it costs. Unfortunately, program integrity type activities are expensive. They are labor intensive. There are just a certain number of things you can do by computer mass sorting of data. You finally have to get to the human elements and get into some judgments as to whether there is really a problem and if there is, how to attack it. (Personal interview).

Budget cuts to the intermediaries directly affect the likelihood that fraudulent and abusive doctors will be caught and punished. It is the intermediaries who have primary responsibility for identifying suspect physicians. The rest of the enforcement system is predicated on a supply of cases coming from hem. Their functions, in terms of identifying potential fraud and abuse are, therefore, important in determining the system's capacity to punish criminal behavior by physicians.

In order to increase the possibility that physicians' hidden crimes were uncovered, intermediaries, at one time, informed patients of the bills that health care providers submitted for services rendered to the beneficiary. However, relatively few cases resulted. Patients may not have looked at the notifications or understood the procedures listed. Or, if they did recognize an improper charge, they may not have reported it. The use of such notifications has greatly declined in recent years (personal interview).

Another avenue for uncovering physician fraud is that of computer screening. Characteristics of physician practices are arrayed, and providers who are more than two standard deviations removed from the mean are "red-flagged" for further investigation. Characteristics of a physician practice which are scrutinized include such items as visits per patient, procedures per patient, and patients per day. These computer screens have limited effectiveness in at they do not accurately pinpoint fraud and abuse. Still, computer usage one of the few ways cases can be generated for investigation; the budget cuts that have decreased fraud and abuse activity have greatly limited the finances that cases generated by computer screening will be investigated. A federal official explains:

> Take the universe of 15,000 doctors such as in New York. They can still identify 450 aberrant doctors every year. It hasn't decreased. However, they can only work each year on less and less as the budget calls for less and less. But because they are working on 50 cases this year—while last year they were working on 100—doesn't mean that there are 50 less aberrant doctors out there. (Personal interview).

Facing severe budget restrictions, most intermediaries will be unable to develop cases for possible criminal prosecution. Cases that are not "worked" re downgraded to "abuses" and are usually handled within the intermediary. This means that in all but the most blatant criminal cases, the most severe action that will befall an errant physician is full or partial repayment of their ill-gotten funds.

Cases that are worked for possible criminal prosecution provide great difficulties for investigators who must, at a minimum, establish that a physician intended to defraud the programs. Investigators normally lack expertise in medical nomenclature, many being former law enforcement personnel. The manager of investigations at one of the intermediaries commented:

> The person most likely to be successful in investigating medical fraud is a registered nurse [who is also] a certified public accountant and [who has spent four years with the FBI. (Personal interview).

Obviously, such people, if they exist at all, are few. Physicians are also able to deflect the possibility of criminal action by blaming errant actions on administrative errors with comments such as: "I didn't know that was what my billing clerk was doing. We'll change it right away" (personal interview). The possible criminal intent of the physician is redefined as a "business error." The criminal investigator, unable to prove otherwise, drops the case.

Tightrope enforcement

Some efforts have been made in the last decade to increase investigative resources. In 1976, the Office of Inspector General

(OIG) was created within the U.S. Department of Health and Human Services to ensure the integrity of government health programs. Under the Reagan administration, the OIG has turned toward an advisory role and away from criminal investigation In addition, criminal prosecutions will be dropped in favor of civil action allowed under the Civil Money Penalties Law signed by President Reagan 1981. Individuals who submit a false claim to Medicare or Medicaid "may be fined up to $2,000 for each improper claim and an additional assessment up to twice the fraudulently claimed amounts" (Office of Inspector General 1983). Such measures, however, insure that fewer cases are taken down the hard road of criminal prosecution.

Also, in 1976, Congress established partial funding for state Medicaid Fraud Control Units (MFCUs). Prior to these units, the states initiated most no criminal prosecutions for violations regarding Medicaid. Most of the financing for Medicaid was from federal dollars. The states lacked the desire to spend their own tax revenues to protect federal monies. Concomitantly the federal government was disinclined to become involved in the enforcement of largely state-run programs. For example, it was not until 1976 that a full time position was created at the federal level to oversee enforcement of the Medicaid program.

As an incentive to the states to establish MFCUs, Congress agreed provide 90 percent funding for the first three years of operation of such units with the state picking up 25 percent of the tab after that. Currently, about 30 states have MFCUs as some states start up units while others cease participation.

A number of factors, however, limit the effectiveness of these and other enforcement units not the least of which is the government's fear of alienating the medical profession through the use of regulatory sanctions and criminal punishment, and thereby reducing the number of physicians participating in the programs. Such considerations are reflected in early decisions regarding the programs. When Medicare and Medicaid were signed into law in 1965 by President Lyndon Johnson, concern for fraud and abuse by physicians was not evidenced in the legislation. Rather, the newly emerging programs were faced with the possibility of a wholesale lack of participation by physicians. The AMA had for years opposed legislation designed to provide government supported medical aid to all of the elderly. Such legislation, the AMA argued, should be based on ability to pay. Medicare makes no such distinction and bases eligibility on age alone. The AMA's outright opposition to Medicare was a rare stance for the organization. Normally, the AMA attempts compromise. The passage of the law was, therefore, a defeat for the AMA (personal interview). Government officials were concerned that doctors might not participate in a program they did not support. Fear of non- participation was real. Lyndon Johnson, for example, authorized the use of veteran's hospitals for any elderly denied treatment (Cohen, 1980).

Another long-standing concern of program administrators with fraud and abuse efforts is the undermining of public confidence in Medicare/ Medicaid. Officials are worried about the delivery of services to the Medicare and Medicaid population. Stories of fraud and abuse by health care providers might weaken funding and slow or reverse the acceptability and applicability of the programs. Rather, administrators wish such accounts hushed (Pontell et al., 1984). The situation is reflected in the words of a high-ranking state official working criminal cases commenting on his counterpart in the state health department:

> The problem is that he is working within an agency whose whole philosophy is to give away. Give away the health care to the poor people and give away the payments to the doctors so they don't make a ruckus. Pay them. Don't hold things up. (Personal interview).

The government, when writing the rules and regulations for Medicare/ Medicaid, adopted many of the medical profession's definitions to encourage doctor participation in the program. Government investigations into fraudulent behavior by doctors violates one of these definitions and create antagonisms between the medical profession and the government program: Physicians tend to see themselves as a "cut above" others (Freidson 1970). The physician, it has traditionally been argued, is guided by a set vice orientation (Abbott, 1983; Parsons, 1951). That is, the physician is more interested in the health of his patient than in any pecuniary reward. Under this viewpoint, safeguards against self-aggrandizement are not as necessary as they might be with other groups. Trust in the profession is further enriched by their training in an esoteric field of knowledge. The physician and only the physician, the professional holds, have the knowledge to diagnose, treat, and prescribe for the patient. Rules and regulations regarding treatment procedures undermine this trust by intruding on the traditional autonomy enjoyed by physicians. Further, it can be argued that the physician must sometimes take chances in treatment. The physician is seen a dealing in life and death situations. Detailed procedures, they argue, will not fit every case. Rather, the patient is asked to trust the doctor's action:

Early attempts by the government to establish rules and regulations were often met by AMA arguments stressing the trust ethic. For example:

> When the law was originally written, it was that he [the physician] had to certify this before the patient got admitted to the hospital, and recertify it after a certain length of time so that there would be somebody's signature there authorizing continuing payment of a hospital bill, and we [the AMA] argued that past procedures in the medical profession in the hospitals —the fact that you had admitted a patient to the hospital — was considered evidence that you thought he should be in the hospital. This seems reasonable, and for once a reasonable argument won out, so that the initial certification got dropped from the law, but the recertification was retained. (Personal interview).

Physicians' view of their profession as self-regulating rejects bureaucratically based policing efforts as unnecessary. Criminal investigations represent an affront to the profession. Thus, this structurally based conflict dictate that the government practice a form of "tightrope enforcement" so as not to decrease the number of physicians who participate in the programs. Investigators must attempt to prove criminal actions but, at the same time not offend the profession as a whole. As a result, many investigatory too have not been widely used. For example, "shopping"—where agents pose as patients—is an effective method for uncovering the hidden criminality of physicians and providing strong evidence of such acts. Yet, few states employ such practices for fear of antagonizing the profession. Investigators are effectively stymied from establishing the means necessary to prove a criminal case in all but the most blatant of crimes. A high-ranking federal official commented:

> There is a group of profiteers, and we hedge because we don't want to offend the powerful medical lobby. But they are absolute crooks and many things that we label as abuse are really fraudulent, but we can't prove intent. (Personal interview).

Taking doctors to court

For physician behavior to be treated criminally requires that prosecutors believe conviction is likely. Prosecutors, however, recognize that as with other white-collar criminals, physicians are a difficult group to "pin a rap on."

Physicians are many times able to cast shady actions in a positive light. For example, providers who knowingly bill for unnecessary services can argue that the procedures were necessary for the health of a patient. Since medicine is not an exact science, and there is much difference among physicians in diagnosis and treatment, it is impossible for a prosecutor to prove beyond a reasonable doubt that a doctor knowingly ordered unnecessary tests in order to defraud the program. Cases of over-utilization are never handled criminally.

Cases that are accepted by the prosecutor for trial almost always involve billing for services never rendered. Doctors who have billed for complex services while on vacation and who have billed for psychiatric services when, in truth, they were having sex with the client, represent cases in which prosecutors were able to successfully prove that the physician intended to defraud the government programs.

Provable guilt is only one factor, however, that goes into a prosecutor's decision to criminally pursue a case. Large dollar losses, according to investigators and prosecutors, are necessary before a criminal charge would be filed against a physician. An investigator commented:

> The first thing they [prosecutors] always look at is money. You can get a guy whose [fraudulent] Medicare bills are $3,000 or $4,000 a year. No matter how good the complaint is, it's probably not going to warrant federal prosecution. (Personal interview).

Proving high dollar loss is often labor intensive. For example, a physician may fraudulently bill the government a few dollars for each patient. The task of reviewing thousands of bills and talking to the beneficiaries prove too much for an already beleaguered investigatory staff.

In addition, most prosecutors lack the expertise to try a case against physician. "Street crime" remains their forte, and few will spend the effort to learn the necessary information, particularly since they realize that the chances of obtaining victory are slim. Some MFCUs attempt to use their own prosecutors to handle cases and thus assure some expertise, but most state and federal cases must rely on young, relatively inexperienced prosecutor. In contrast, the physician is able to use his comparatively ample resources to hire a highly skilled defense attorney.

Prosecutors also feel that judges do not welcome physician cases as they require them to learn complex material and may clog the court calendar Juries, as well, are believed by the prosecutor to be ignorant of physician malfeasance and tend to favor the defendant as a member of a prestigious group. "No one would suspect this upstanding pillar of the community of any fraudulent intent. He doesn't look like the average criminal. He has a tremendous education, makes a great appearance" (personal interview Research by Rosoff (1984), however, has suggested that physicians as criminal defendants may suffer from "status liability" and thus be more likely to be convicted and receive a longer sentence than other individuals employed in slightly less prestigious occupations. This effect was demonstrated whet the evidence against the defendant was "overwhelming," however, which represents only a minority of physician fraud cases.

Actual cases that have resulted in jail or prison sentences are rare; the bias is to see the conviction of the physician and the accompanying loss status as punishment enough. Serving time, as well, may remove needed medical services from an undeserving population:

> There was a case in Philadelphia [of a doctor) who got nailed for the third time. The first time it was for IRS fraud. The second time it was Medicaid, and then he came up a third time on Medicare. When the doctor showed up to be sentenced, he brought in his Medicare population who were going to be disadvantaged by his being gone. So the judge came up with a fairly creative sentence. He gave him weekends. The guy practiced during the week, and on weekends, we assume, he went to jail. (Personal interview).

Prosecutors only accept cases that can reasonably be expected to result in conviction. Past experience has taught them to "go slowly." Prosecutors are cautious because they believe judges and juries unwilling to convict physicians unless criminal behavior is egregious. In addition, "fellow feeling" based on shared backgrounds and world views render it difficult to distinguish the offender distinctly from the enforcer. Sutherland (1983) insisted that the status and lifestyle homogeneity between government officials and affluent, well placed white-collar criminals, was in considerable measure responsible for the comparable leniency with which these law violators were treated in those relatively rare incidences when their cases proceeded as far as trial and sentencing. Sutherland also suggested that the violations of white-collar offenders were quite "understandable" to figures such as judges; in many instances, they themselves have been guilty of similar kinds of illegal behavior as part of their own occupational incumbency.

Judges, for instance, may well have to play fast and loose with campaign contribution laws in order to gain their election victory or political appointment. A high ranking federal official's attitude about judges and the possibility of jail time for doctors is aptly explained:

> For a long time I was hard-nosed. When we convicted a guy I wanted to see him do hard time. But what the hell seeing what's going on in prisons these days and things like that, I think to put one of these guys in prison for hard time doesn't make any sense; but if we can nail them financially, if we can impact upon the way they live and the profits they reaped from that type of thing by taking away—if necessary—their homes, or their nice bank accounts, then I think we'd be a helluva lot better off than if we put them in jail for six months... And the judges just find ways to make sure they don't do hard time. (Personal interview).

All of the above, combined with the possibility that the defendant may well be politically influential and affect the reelection chances of the prosecutor, put a severe damper on prosecutorial zeal in regard to physician fraud. Cases that are not accepted by the prosecutor are referred back to the health department, intermediary or carrier for civil or administrative action. The doctor may face repayment of funds and a requirement that all future services be approved for payment in advance or possible suspension from billing Medicaid or Medicare, but public knowledge of the criminal ac will be largely limited and any substantial effect unlikely:

> You never can get any doctor de-licensed for being a thief. They won't take his license away for being a thief, because that really has nothing to do with his expertise. If he did something wrong to the patient, the fixing of the patient, that is something else altogether. As far as being a thief, over-billing, double-billing, services not rendered, forget it. It never really gets to the heart of kicking him out. They can kick him out of Medicaid, but who the hell cares about Medicaid. The guy's still making bucks. (Personal interview).

Discussion: physicians and punishment

A number of authors have suggested that the traditional logic for punishments is more applicable to white-collar criminals than to street offender (Chambliss, 1967; Geis, 1973; President's Crime Commission, 1967; Braithwaite, 1982). Braithwaite and Geis (1982:311), for example, have argue that "crime control by public disgrace, deterrence, incapacitation, and rehabilitation could be highly successful when applied to corporate criminals Such beliefs inevitably have to rest on the assumption that sanctions can be effectively applied to white-collar criminals.

This paper has argued that limits to the application of sanctions to physician offenders negate the possibility of securing crime control by punishment. Punishment, where it exists at all, usually boils down to a hand slap or repayment of funds and less than what might be considered a major inconvenience. Such sanctioning is not without merit. It may have a moralizing educative effect on physicians (Andenaes, 1970). Unaware of parameters, they practice as they see fit. Once notified, however, they might quickly conform. But lacking knowledge of such sanctions, other physicians who practice the same way as the punished individual will continue to treat in a. similar manner.

Punishment may also act as a specific deterrent. The violator may feel the sting of the penalty, conclude that the potential cost of wrongdoing too high, and conform to avoid future punishments. In this regard, a federal enforcement official noted that "doctors' earnings go down when they realize they are being investigated" (personal interview). Such sanctions, however probably do not come to the attention of the vast majority of physicians (Freidson, 1975), and thus have little effect as a general deterrent. Rehabilitation, long considered a failure for street criminals (Martinson, 1974), is the criterion for punishment most stressed by those sympathetic to the medical profession. A state official noted:

> We don't try to be exclusively punitive. We don't measure our success by how much money we get back for the state. We think a large part of what we do should be educational and working with the profession. (Personal interview).

Since few physicians are identified or sanctioned as fraudulent, it is unlikely that the vast majority of errant physicians can be controlled by punishment. Methods, other than law enforcement, may prove far more satisfactory as a limit to criminal activity.

A basic cornerstone of any punishment doctrine is the necessity that the majority of the public support the law and the sanctions imposed for violation of that law. Deterrence, for example, is based on social contract or consensus theory. A person's continual presence in society is viewed as voluntary. One chooses, under this model, to accept the rules of the general society and to give up some individual freedoms as a result. The law, for the most part, must be acceptable to the society. Attempts to implement laws that are not acceptable, risk the danger of dwindling to state oppression. In a free society, one must stop short of such measures. If the people find enforcement to be unacceptable, the law will have much less of a deterrent effect. In addition, the law will lack a moral influence. As Andenaes (1975:363) notes: "The law and the machinery for enforcement of it must be looked upon as wielding legitimate authority."

A lack of public consensus regarding the law and its sanctions prevent the implementation of punishment. Social contract theory today is largely a myth (as it may well have been when it was first enunciated). Each individual's participation in society can be considered to be largely involuntary. That is, one is born into a society, and by learning its norms, values and customs, has little opportunity to adjust to any other type of situation. In addition, a belief in a consensus model of society has been deeply eroded. Some see the law as little more than a tool of the ruling elite. Laws, rather than reflecting a consensus, are seen as shaped by the powerful (Kolko, 1962; Turk, 1969; Quinney, 1974).

In regard to fraud in Medicare/Medicaid, physicians offer a unique opportunity for studying the effects of legitimacy of government rules on participants' behavior. Program regulations negatively affect participation by physicians (Mitchell and Cromwell, 1982). In addition, dissatisfaction with repayment by the government has been suggested as a factor increasing fraud and abuse against the programs (Pontell, et al., 1984). Some physicians over utilize, charge for services never rendered, and commit other illegal act to make back some of the monies that they believe is rightfully due them We can assume that if too many of the rules and regulations of Medicare/ Medicaid are unacceptable to physicians, they will not participate. Given the power of the medical profession and the structure of medical practice, it is extremely difficult to implement penalties. To the extent that this is true it will be equally difficult to affect physician behavior through punishment.

Conclusion

The present paper illustrates a number of things about the punishment and control of white-collar crime. It suggests, on the basis of its review of Medicare and Medicaid violations by physicians, that a strong profession can insulate itself from effective legal action against its members. In part, this is because of professional power; in part, it is because the laws and rule violated are impossible to enforce stringently with resources allocated any probably with any kind of reasonable resources. There might be improve detection in the future, but only a change in the structure of the program will significantly alter the level of violations. Computers ultimately will see to it that interest payments from banks show up on taxpayers' returns, but there is little way to monitor underground cash payments. So, too, will doctors be able to over utilize for personal profit until they become salaried employees. Though absolute control of most any crime is well beyond enforcement ability, the story of medical fraud and abuse adds to the argument that white-collar offenders benefit from a policy of benign neglect, largely traceable to their ability to impose their own definitions of control upon those who might be in a position to impose tougher regulation.

*This research was supported by a grant from the National Institute of Justice, U.S. Department of Justice (82-IJ-CX-0035) and a grant-in-aid from Indiana University, Bloomigton. The views expressed are those of the authors and do not necessarily reflect the positions of the funding bodies. The authors wish to thank Fran Renner and Beth Wininger for typing assistance.

4. Sanctions against corporations: economic efficiency or legal efficacy?

Brent Fisse*

Corporate wrongdoing, in the sense of unlawful conduct committed by on behalf of a company, is a serious social problem of our time. The economic costs alone are massive; by any estimate, they greatly overshadow he economic costs of unlawful conduct by individuals acting on their own behalf. The physical costs of corporate wrongs are also heavy; estimates vary but it seems undeniable that unlawful corporate conduct kills or maims are more people than does unlawful conduct by persons acting on their own account. Furthermore, the speculation is rife that corporate wrongdoing erodes the moral fabric of society; as Edwin Sutherland suggested (in 1949):

> The financial cost from white collar crime, great as it is, is less important than the damage to social relations. White collar crimes violate trust and, therefore, create distrust; this lowers social morale and produces social disorganization.

These perceptions are not elitist academic exaggerations but are shared by many in the general community. Surveys have shown that the once prevalent supposition that corporate illegality is "morally neutral" or merely "economic" does not reflect public opinion. For instance, in one U.S. survey of attitudes toward the seriousness of crimes, a national sample of 8,000 respondents rated white collar crimes involving injury to persons (e.g., lethal toxic waste pollution) as extremely serious, and more so than many main street offenses (including robbery with violence). In addition to the result of this and other polls, there have been numerous outcries over actual or alleged corporate offenses. The Bhopal disaster, the Seveso scandal, the Pentagon defense contract swindles, the Kepone affair, and the Ford Pinto allegations are merely a few of the incidents in recent history which have aroused widespread public resentment toward questionable corporate behavior.

Serious as unlawful corporate harm doing or risk taking often is, the response in law frequently amounts to a rap on the knuckles. In the ever of a successful prosecution being mounted, the sentence is typically a low fine. This is true even in an area such as industrial health and safety when death and serious injury are at stake. In numerous cases where an industrial safety violation has resulted in death or severe injury the sanction imposed on the company has been a paltry fine or monetary penalty. Remarkably, the fines imposed for antitrust violations and consumer protection offenses have usually been much higher. Nonetheless, a cash punishment amounting to say 5-10% of the annual profits of a corporate offender pale into insignificance when compared with the severity of the sanctions which can be and often are imposed on individuals for street offenses. Apart from the inegalitarianism of this approach, it seems fanciful to suppose that fines or monetary penalties at the level now typically imposed on companies provide a cogent deterrent threat. Thus, a recent study of antitrust penalties under the Australian Trade Practices Act led its author to this conclusion:

Deterrence can only be effectively provided if the courts are prepared to impose heavy penalties. Corporate executives may only be deterred from engaging in anti-competitive conduct if they face a realistic prospect of very large penalties, or if some social stigma is attached to being found guilty of antitrust offenses. Unfortunately, there is scant evidence that all these requirements are being presently met in the enforcement of the Australian antitrust legislation.

If more effective sanctions against corporate wrongdoing are needed, what exactly should be done to re-arm the law? A proposal current in the United States and abroad is that we should develop a regime of monetary penalties based on the canon of economic efficiency. Under this approach, corporate offenders would be punished according to a calculus aimed at achieving the "biggest bang" for the enforcement buck. According to this calculus, monetary penalties are usually taken to be the least costly and hence optimal means of controlling crime. Numerous equations for ascertaining the optimal type and amount of punishment have been formulated of varying degrees of sophistication. One important feature is that the level of punishment costs should be geared not merely to the loss or gain flowing from an offense, but to the probability of detection and conviction; a 10% chance of detection and conviction would result in a punishment cost 10 times higher than if the probability of detection and conviction were 1. On this theme there are many variations, including the per se formula put forward by Kenneth Elzinga and William Breit in their leading work, The Antitrust Penalties. According to Elzinga and Breit, antitrust violations should be penalized by a mandatory penalty of 25% of a firm's pre-tax profits for every year of anti-competitive activity.

The argument of the essay presented here is that economic efficiency is unsatisfactory as a guide to the development of more effective sanctions against corporations. First, monetary exaction is an inept means of punishment in many ways, including its inability to pinch directly on the managerial nerves of corporate governance, and its proneness to inflict over spills on innocent workers, shareholders and consumers. Second, corporations conceivably can be punished otherwise than by means of fines and the more promising possible additional forms of sanction—stock dilution (equity fines), probation and punitive injunctions, publicity orders, and community service orders—seem capable of overcoming the worst limitations of monetary punishment. Third, attractive as the canon of economic efficiency may be, it has several inegalitarian tendencies if used as a foundation for the design of sanctions against corporations.

Limitations of fines and monetary penalties

We now rely very heavily on fines or civil monetary penalties as the means of sanctioning corporate violators. Although fines or monetary penalties are advantageous in some important respects (notably ease of administration, noninterference in the internal affairs of corporations, and contribution toward the costs of enforcement), they are subject to a number of limitations which are reviewed below. These limitations are significant and impel a search for additional forms of sanction.

Limited punitive impact

It is often said that the only major weakness of fines or monetary penalties against corporations is that courts and legislatures have not been willing to set them high enough to provide a real deterrent. The solution, according to many commentators, is to follow the canon of economic efficiency by providing for and applying much higher fines or monetary penalties. This solution is problematical because the potential punitive impact of monetary punishment is necessarily limited by the extent to which money can count as a deterrent, retributive or rehabilitative factor in the control of corporate wrongdoing.

An initial limitation of monetary punishment is that corporate defendants often do not have the resources to pay fines or monetary penalties in the amount theoretically required for effective deterrence. As John C. Coffee, Jr. has explained, fines against corporations are confronted by a "deterrence trap:"

The maximum meaningful fine that can be levied against any corporate offender is necessarily bounded by its wealth. Logically, a small corporation is no more threatened by a $5 million fine than by a $500,000 fine if both are beyond its ability to pay. In short, our ability to deter the corporation may be confounded by our inability to set an adequate punishment cost which does not exceed the corporation's resources.

Similarly, from the standpoint of retribution, the fine warranted by an offense may be much larger than a corporate defendant is able to pay. We then face what may be called a "retribution trap." This problem has been raised by John Braithwaite:

> [Can] we imagine any penalty short of revoking the corporation's right to sell drugs which would be commensurate to the harm caused by the fraud and deceit of a thalidomide disaster? Given what we know about how disapproving the community feels toward corporate crime, there may be many situations where the deserved monetary or other punishment bankrupts the company. The community then cuts off its nose to spite its face.

Another significant limitation is that cash fines or penalties against corporations pose a monetary threat which is not well tuned to the non-financial values that partly govern organizational decision making. Although it often said that corporate activity is normally undertaken to reap some economic benefit and that corporate decision makers choose courses of action based on a calculation of financial costs and benefits, non-financial value are also important. Managerial motivation, like human motivation in general, is not confined to satisfaction of monetary want but includes the urge for power, the desire for prestige, the creative urge, and the need for security Since fines or monetary penalties against corporations touch upon these non-monetary managerial motivations only obliquely, their sanctioning capacity is restricted. Furthermore, although profit may be the predominant goal of business corporations from an external viewpoint, the profit goal is often overshadowed within a corporation by the more immediate goals of organizational sub-units. This phenomenon has been well described by Christophe Stone:

> As corporations become more complex, they tend to subdivide into various departments according to geographical divisions (manufacturing areas and distribution territories), functioning defined groups (finance, sales, advertising, legal) ... The central organization cannot leave each of those groups at large to realize 'profit goal' as it sees best. Rather, the farther and farther down the operational ladder one moves, the more the 'profit goal' has to be translated into sub-goals—targets and objectives for the shop, the department, the plant, the division, the subsidiary. It is these sub-goals that define the task environment of the people actually engaged in production at such a plant, not some abstract `corporate profit.'

It should also be remembered that corporate personnel conceive their own ends in terms which may diverge substantially from the goals of their corporation or its organizational sub-units. For instance, lower management may falsify pollution compliance reports to avoid closure of an obsolete plant, not so much to maximize profits for the firm as to save their own jobs or reputation in the local community.

Devaluation of the gravity of corporate crime

One of the traditional hallmarks of the criminal law has been the stress placed on the socially-unwanted nature of offenses. From the standpoint of both deterrence and retribution, reliance has been placed on the technique of denouncing certain forms of conduct as wrong and un-purchasable even if he offender has the capacity to provide monetary redress. Given that many kinds of corporate offenses are patently unwanted by the community, it seems insensitive to make fines available as the only punitive sanction for such offenses. Fines do not emphatically convey the message that serious offenses are unwanted. Rather, the impression fostered is that the commission of rime is permissible provided there is willingness to pay the going price.

Murder, manslaughter, theft and at least all the more serious offense protect interests which transcend monetary value and this is one reason why provision has been made for jail and other non-monetary forms of punishment. The provision of jail, community service and probation as sentencing options in addition to that of the fine signifies that the offense is not merely "economic crime"

which can be purchased by payment of a fine but unwanted behavior which society has denounced and prohibited.

Consider the infamous cost-benefit analysis which the Ford
Motor Company allegedly used in designing the fuel tank system
of the Pinto subcompact (the car "that carried death in the boot').
The allegation, will be recalled, was that Ford callously chose not
to make "an $11-per-car improvement that would prevent 180 fiery
deaths a year." The intense public hostility expressed against Ford in
relation to this episode revealed an understandable antipathy to the
notion that human lives should be valued simply in terms of
money. Yet what if Ford had in fact been convicted unlawful
homicide? Merely to have fined the company would have
reduced the law to making a simplistic and insensitive monetary
evaluation of much the same kind as that for which Ford had been
condemned by the general public.

Compromise of individual accountability

An additional consideration is that fines or monetary penalties
against corporations target at the corporate entity and not the
personnel who should be held individually accountable for the
offense involved. This would matter little if any personnel at fault
were proceeded against criminally or eve civilly, but proceedings
against corporate officers or employees are not always brought.
Given the limited resources of enforcement agencies seems
inevitable that the targets of prosecution will often be corporation
and that individual accountability frequently will be attainable
only by pressuring corporate defendants to take internal
disciplinary measures. Fines or monetary penalties poorly reflect
this strategy of enforced self-discipline since they provide no
guarantee that a corporate defendant will in fact take disciplinary
action. Moreover, corporations have incentives which tend to
inhibit disciplinary reaction. A disciplinary program may be too
disruptive, too embarrassing for those exercising managerial
control, or too fertile a source of evidence for subsequent civil
litigation against the company or its officers. In short, the impact
of enforcement can easily stop with a corporate pay-out, not because
of any socially justified departure from the traditional value of
individual accountability, but rather because that is the cheapest or
most self-protective course for a corporate defendant to adopt.

The ease with which fines against corporations can be used to
sell out individual accountability is illustrated by the deal struck
in 1981 to settle the McDonnell-Douglas bribery affair with Pak-

istani Airlines. Fraud and conspiracy charges against four top McDonnell-Douglas executives were dropped in return for a guilty plea by the company to charges of fraud and making false statements. Under the plea agreement McDonnell incurred a fine of $55,000 and agreed to pay $1.2 million in civil damages. This deal was struck at a meeting between the U.S. Associate Attorney General and representatives of McDonnell-Douglas. The prosecutors in the case (who had not been invited to the meeting and subsequently resigned from the Justice Department) were of the view that the liability of the four executives had been "bought off" by the settlement.

Non-assurance of responsive corporate reform

In theory, fines or monetary penalties against corporations are supposed to catalyze reform of organizational compliance systems, but in practice change need not occur.

Corporate managers may decide to treat fines as recurrent business losses for shareholders or workers to bear. Depending upon competitive pressures, those losses might also be passed onto consumers. Preventive procedures or policies may be revised, but there is no obligation to react in this way, even when the offense subject to sentence resulted from palpably defective organizational controls.

Instructive in this regard are the findings of Hopkins' valuable empirical study of the impact of prosecutions and fines under the Australian Trade Practices Act. In the 17 case histories of misleading advertising studied, the offenses committed by 15 of the companies were interpreted as largely attributable to defective standard operating procedures after prosecution. Nine of these 15 companies changed their operating procedures accordingly. Two made minor changes which were less than fully satisfactory. Two further companies made no changes and for the two remaining companies information was unavailable. The conclusion drawn by Hopkins was that:

> [w]here defective operating procedures were involved ... the prosecution can be said to have led to significant organizational improvement in at least 60 percent of cases. On the face of it the prosecutions have had a substantial preventive effect on the companies concerned.

However, in approximately 40 percent of the cases studied, the companies concerned failed to provide a responsive program of organizational reform. The further conclusion may thus be drawn that fines or monetary penalties may maximize corporate freedom by trusting corporations to exercise adequate internal control, but they are inept where companies cannot be trusted to institute adequate crime-preventive controls.

Loss-minimization via subsidiaries

Account must also be taken of the potential vulnerability of fines to loss minimization through the use of subsidiary corporations as a cushion. B3 operating through subsidiaries, large enterprises can exploit the principle that an incorporated subsidiary is a distinct legal entity from its parent or holding company. Under the principle of separate corporate identity, subsidiary is answerable only for its own conduct and any fine imposed or a subsidiary is assessed by reference to its own financial state and not that of the parent or holding company.

This stratagem for cushioning the impact of fines became notorious when shortly after the turn of the century, Judge Landis unsuccessfully attempted to fine Standard Oil $29 million for illegal freight charge rebating. Landis maintained that the defendant, the Standard Oil Co. of Indiana, was a puppet of the giant Standard Oil Co. of New Jersey, and he expressly geared the $29 million fine to the financial resources and compliance performance or the parent company. On appeal, the fine was struck down as manifestly excessive because the defendant was not the parent, Standard Oil of New Jersey, but the subsidiary, Standard Oil of Indiana.

The distinct legal status of incorporated subsidiaries continues to obstruct the effective administration of fines. One example is the Browning Arms case in Canada in the mid-seventies. The fully-owned local subsidiary, a company with a turnover of $C140,000, was convicted of resale price maintenance and fined $C60,000. On appeal, the fine was reduced to $C10,000. For the parent U.S. company, which had a turnover of $C55 million, this fine was hardly a punishment which jolted the conscience, but a minor expense of doing business in Canada.

One response to this problem is to pierce the corporate veil by statute and to enable fines to be assessed according to some index of the financial resources of the overall enterprise. Under the European Economic Community antitrust laws, fines may run up to 10% of the offending company's previous year's turnover. In the case of multinationals, the fine can be based on the world turnover of the enterprise, not just the turnover generated within the EEC by a local subsidiary.

However, this is an imperfect solution. Fines are ultimately enforceable by seizing the defendant's assets. Thus, the enforceability of a large fine based on the global turnover of a multinational is governed by the extent of the assets of the local subsidiary and usually these are relatively small. And even where those assets are sufficient to cover such a fine, enforcing payment may drive the local operation out of business, with disastrous effects on workers and trade creditors.

Overspills

It is notorious that fines or monetary penalties can inflict unacceptable overspills on innocent shareholders, consumers and workers.

A long-standing objection to fines against corporations is that their impact within the firm falls unjustly on shareholders (through reduced dividends or lower share prices) rather than on managers. Managers are usually much better positioned than shareholders to exert control over corporate harm doing or risk taking and so should bear the greater burden of fines. The managers bear the greater burden only if they happen to hold the bulk of the corporate offender's shares. In companies of any size this is rarely the case.

The problem of spillovers of fines onto consumers and workers is also well known. Depending on the characteristics of the relevant market, heavily fining a corporation may lead to consumer price hikes, worker layoffs, increase resistance to demands for higher wages, and other damage to hapless third parties. When General Motors catches a cold, so it is still said, the world sneezes.

Conclusion as regards limitations of cash punishment

Fines and monetary penalties, as assessed above, have many limitations as sanctions against corporations. However, these limitations should not 13, overstated.

A conviction itself, regardless of the form of sentence, can have significant deterrent, retributive or rehabilitative value. Convictions strike at the desire for prestige and power within organizations and signal the need for critical self-reappraisal and correction. Furthermore, condemning a corporation by means of conviction imposes a stigma which, unlike monetary loss cannot simply be written off as a business cost or passed on to others. The impact of convictions alone, however, is limited. Corporate convictions are often not publicized through either the news media or through the convicted corporation's own channels of communication. Moreover, even if news of conviction did lead to a scandal, there is no guarantee that the company concerned would react by undertaking a program of responsive internal discipline or organizational reform.

Another consideration which is important in practice is the impact of legal costs; these can and often do exceed the amount of the fine or monetary penalty imposed. For this reason, it has sometimes been urged that there is no need to introduce additional forms of sanction against corporations However, this contention may be rejected, on two main grounds. First, the impact of legal costs is often high for those who defend themselves against charges of manslaughter, theft, or attempting to pervert the course of justice and yet this consideration has not been regarded as a sufficient reason for making such offenses subject to punishment only by means of a fine. Second, where heavy legal costs have been incurred, that factor could be taken into account in mitigation of sentence; if so, the appropriate sentence might not necessarily be further monetary exaction but a non-monetary punishment such as community service.

Additional sanctions against corporations: their potential for overcoming the limitations of fines

What additional forms of sanction against corporations might be used? Dissolution, disqualification from government contracts, production bans, and other forms of incapacitation have often been made available but, whatever the possible attraction of any analogy to imprisonment, these forms of sanction are extreme and, if used, can easily cause worse side-effects (e. g. layoffs of workers) than the harm prevented. There are more promising possibilities, however, namely stock dilution (equity fines), probation and punitive injunctions, publicity orders, and community service orders. These alternatives are now outlined together with their main potential advantages over fines.

Stock dilution (equity fines)

One possible alternative to fines or monetary penalties is stock dilution, an imaginative approach recently proposed by John C. Coffee, Jr. The proposal, in essence, is this:

> [W]hen very severe fines need to be imposed on the corporation, they should be imposed not in cash, but in the securities of the corporation. The convicted corporation should be required to authorize and issue such number of shares to the state's crime victim compensation fund as would have an expected market value equal to the cash fine necessary to deter illegal activity. The fund should then be able to liquidate the securities in whatever manner maximizes its return.

This proposal could be fine-tuned to advantage in various ways, as by providing for a statutory list of appropriate beneficiaries of the shares create (e.g. in the context of environmental offenses, conservation foundations, for consumer protection offenses, consumer organizations) but the basic idea-watering down shares rather than exacting money—is a classically straight forward instance of lateral thinking.

One advantage of stock dilution, as compared with cash fines or monetary penalties, is that they would side-step the deterrence or retribution trap which arises when the wealth of a corporation places an upper limit on monetary punishment, and where this upper limit is less than the amour required to deter or requite corporate crime. To put the point simply, by appropriating fixed as well as liquid assets, the sanction of stock dilution raises the upper limit of the amount collectible. Moreover, the upper limit is raised further by the capacity of stock dilution to reach future assets in addition to current assets. The public seizes not just whatever cash the company can find to pay a fine or monetary penalty but a share in future earnings as well as ownership rights in its plant, equipment, and property investments. The basic explanation for this, as Coffee has indicated, is that the market valuation of most companies vastly exceeds their cash resources:

> The equity fine is a response to the basic precept of the economist that the value of the firm is the discounted present value of its expected future earnings. An equity fine permits society to reach its future earnings today by seizing a share of the firm's equity (which is, of course, equal in value to the market's perception of the discounted present value of those earnings)

Another advantage of stock dilution over a fine or monetary penalty that the problem of overspills to workers and consumers would be reduced. Stock dilution (equity fines) would not occasion these unwanted spillovers; shareholders would bear the burden just as other losses are borne by them when the company in which they have invested is unsuccessful. A limitation of this type of sanction is that the impact of equity fines falls on all shareholders and does not discriminate between those who wield managerial control and those who are merely relatively powerless outsiders.

Useful as punitive stock dilution orders would be as a means of outflanking the deterrence and retribution traps, standing alone they could not be expected to overcome other major limitations of fines or monetary penalties against corporations. Above all, they would not be capable of overcoming the following limitations: lack of congruence with non-financial values in organizational decision making, compromise of individual accountability, and non-assurance of responsive corporate reform.

As regards congruence with non-financial values in organizational decision making, dilution of stock value could have some adverse effects upon corporate and managerial prestige and power, yet the punitive impact would remain predominantly financial. Coffee has urged that equity fines would play on managerial fear of hostile takeover bids, on the basis that vesting a large marketable block of shares in a free agent such as a crime victim compensation fund would make a corporation a more inviting target for a takeover operation. However, the block of shares created by an equity fine would normally have to be very large to create any serious risk of takeover for a large company.

Equity fines might help to promote individual accountability to some extent but this effect would not necessarily occur. Equity fines would make a more significant impression on shareholders than would cash fines or penalties and hence securities analysts and stockbrokers might begin to caution against buying into companies with inadequate compliance systems. Moreover, if severe equity fines were in fact imposed, shareholders might also insist upon internal disciplinary action by management. Thus, there could be more chance that punishing the corporate entity would result in the disciplining of individuals within the organization. However, there would be no guarantee of this. Shareholders might still decide to cut their losses and let managers pursue their business or, as another option, exit towards other investment opportunities instead of remaining to express their voice.

Nor would stock dilution ensure that corporate defendants take adequate organizational precautions against re-offending. By reason of the greater possible severity of equity fines, corporations could be put under more pressure to take such precautions, but that increase in pressure would stop short of

intervention by the state in the internal workings of the organization. Accordingly, like cash fines or penalties, punitive stock
dilution orders would not guarantee the correction of violation-
prone procedures or policies. The organization would remain a
black box prodded by the law only from outside.

Probation and punitive injunctions

Although it is sometimes said that corporations are inappropriate
subject for rehabilitation, this overlooks corporate probation, a
sentence use increasingly in the United States. Several proposals
have now been advance for the more extensive utilization of this
option, probation being a convenient platform upon which to base
a number of more particularized sanctions. Of these more particularized sanctions, the main possibilities are probation orders
mandating internal discipline or organizational reform. And
beyond probation, there is the tougher possible option of the
punitive injunction.

Internal discipline orders have been advocated by the Mitchell
Committee in South Australia, the suggestion being as follows:

> Essentially, internal discipline orders would require a corporation
> to investigate an offense committed on its behalf, undertake
> appropriate disciplinary proceedings, and return a detailed and
> satisfactory compliance report to the court issuing the particular
> order. In the event of unreasonable non-compliance corporate
> criminal responsibility would be necessary in some cases, but
> usually it would be sufficient to impose individual criminal
> responsibility on those personnel specified in the order as
> responsible for securing compliance. Unlike the system of
> Frankpledge, the object of internal discipline orders thus would
> not be to produce guilty individuals to the prosecuting
> authorities, but to cast part of the burden of enforcement squarely
> upon the enterprise on whose behalf an offense has been committed.

At first glance, this proposal may seem unworkable in so far as
it would require corporations to confess wrongdoing on the part
of its officers or employees and then administer punishment
itself. However, this reaction seems to overlook the importance
attached to internal discipline throughout the history of corporate
regulation. For instance, enforced internal discipline was exp-
ressly the policy adopted by the Securities and Exchange
Commission in its successful campaign against foreign bribery
during the mid-1970s. Faced with hundreds of likely corporate
violators and thousands of individual suspects, the SEC imp-

lemented a "voluntary disclosure program" which pressurized the corporations into taking internal disciplinary action. The basic strategy underlying such an approach, it should be emphasized, is to make a direct appeal to rational self-interest. If the corporation and its managerial personnel are threatened with severe sanctions in the event of non-compliance, compliance commends itself as the lesser of two evils.

Organizational reform orders have been proposed, under various labels, by a number of reform agencies and commentators. The common emphasis of these proposals is that corporate compliance policies and procedures should be revised under court scrutiny when organizational reform is necessary to guard against repetition of an offense. This approach has recently been recommended under the American Bar Association's Standards for Criminal Justice as Standard 18.2.8(a)(v). These standards allow for continuing judicial oversight over corporate activities, oversight to be implemented:

> ...through the use of recognized reporting, record keeping, and auditing controls designed to increase internal accountability ...
> It shout be noted that the ABA proposal would not require the probation service to assume onerous new duties of corporate supervision. Where supervision is required, reliance would be placed on an experienced corporate attorney, firm of auditors, or a professional director.

An initial question raised by the ABA model is whether it goes far enough toward providing an effective sanction. Probation and continuing judicial oversight are rather benign sanctions. Certainly probation has usually bee] regarded as a soft sentencing option because it is more in the nature of rehabilitative remedy than a deterrent or retributive punishment. Serious cases, it may be argued, call for a more potent sanction which can punish as well as spur internal compliance.

A sanction well-suited for this purpose would be the punitive injunction a variant of the civil mandatory injunction. A punitive injunction could be used not only to require a corporate defendant to revamp its internal controls but also to do so in some punitively demanding way. Instead of requiring a defendant merely to remedy the situation by introducing state of-the-art preventive equipment or procedures, it would be possible to insist on the development of innovative techniques. The punitive injunction could thus serve as both punishment and super-remedy.

If internal discipline and organizational reform orders were available a probationary conditions or punitive injunctions, they would provide a means of overcoming the worst limitations of fines or monetary penalties against corporations.

First, the deterrence or retribution trap which confronts attempts to impose heavy cash fines or penalties could largely be skirted by recourse to internal discipline or organizational reform orders. The deterrent or retributive impact of these sanctions would rest largely on financial or nonfinancial internal disciplinary sanctions and detraction from corporate or managerial power, and these are impacts which, unless carried to extremes, can be borne by corporations without sending them into financial ruin.

Second, internal discipline and organizational reform orders would be much more congruent with non-financial values in organizational decision making. Corporate and managerial power would be affected directly, corporate and managerial prestige would be threatened at least to some extent and the goals of organizational sub-units would be immediately relevant to probationary or injunctive review of a company's compliance procedures.

Third, punitive injunctions, unlike cash or equity fines, would clearly manifest the unwanted nature of serious corporate crime. The message conveyed would be that offenses are not convertible into financial business expenses or share value losses but amount to deprivations of human well-being which, because they are not compensable, are prohibited and preventable by forcible restraint upon corporate choice.

Fourth, internal discipline orders would enable corporate offenders to be sanctioned in such a way as to promote individual accountability for corporate offenses. Unlike fines or monetary penalties, this type of sanction would be targeted directly towards those personnel who were implicated in the offense subject to sentence.

Fifth, as far as catalyzing organizational reform is concerned, probationary conditions or punitive injunctions would provide the most obvious method for insisting that corporate defendants respond adequately to any structural or other institutional problems which have occasioned the commission of an offense. Take the Digital case. Instead of imposing a monetary penalty and hoping for a revitalized compliance effort, it would be possible to require the company to revise its export screening procedures, to use its international facilities to audit the destination of products supplied, to report back to the enforcement agency at periodic intervals and, if necessary, to have those reports verified by an independent monitor.

Sixth, the problem of overspills would be greatly reduced. The dominant impact of probation or punitive injunctions would be interference with managerial power and prestige, not exaction of cash or dilution of the value of shares. Accordingly, the loss inflicted would flow mainly to managers rather than to shareholders, workers or consumers. And instead of making an indiscriminate attack on all managers, it would be possible to target particular managers or classes of manager under the terms of the probationary or injunctive order imposed.

The main question surrounding the prospect of probationary directives and punitive injunctions is whether they could be used without subjecting corporations to inefficient and excessively intrusive governmental intervention. Two answers may be given here. First, we tolerate the high social costs of imprisonment because fines of sufficient deterrent or retributive weight typically cannot be paid by individual offenders. Because we tolerate these costs, the administrative and other costs associated with corporate probation or punitive injunctions may be defended on a similes ground. The deterrent and retributive traps created by the limited wealth of corporations require us either to maintain a crime control system based on cash fines, which cannot be expected to work, or to resort to an alternative means of control which, although regrettably more costly, is more likely to be effective. Second, probation or punitive injunctions could be controller in such a way as to avoid corporations being subjected to any overbearing regime of state control. For one thing, the customary sentencing practice of imposing severe sanctions only for serious offenses is unlikely to be abandoned. For another, sentencing criteria could and should be devised so as to maximize freedom of enterprise in compliance systems. One possibility would be to stipulate in the empowering legislation that, wherever practicable, corporate defendants be given the opportunity to indicate before sentence what disciplinary or other steps they propose to take in response to their conviction for an offense.

Publicity

A third possibility is to make adverse publicity available as a formal court ordered punitive sanction. This form of sanction should be contrasted with merely remedial publicity orders (e. g. corrective advertising orders).

This approach, which goes back to the English Bread Acts of the early nineteenth century, was suggested in 1970 by the U.S. National Commission on Reform of Federal Criminal Laws (the Brown Commission) Section 405 of the Brown Commission's Study Draft provided in relevant part a follows:

> When an organization is convicted of an offense, the court may, in addition to or in lieu of imposing other authorized sanctions ...require the organization to give appropriate publicity to the conviction by notice to the class or classes of persons or sector of the public interested in or affected by the conviction, by advertising in designated areas or by designated media, or ...

This proposal was never implemented. However, the idea has since been revived, partly because of a growing realization that most corporations are highly sensitive about their prestige as an interest over and above (although overlapping with) profits. Apart from the patent relevance of prestige to everyday corporate public relations exercises, the reactions of companies themselves to adverse publicity has been the subject of empirical enquiry in a recent study of the impacts of adverse publicity on 17 major U.S. and Australasian companies. One of the conclusions emerging from this study was that senior executives experienced anguish or at least concern over their perception that corporate prestige had been assaulted by adverse publicity, even when the publicity had no adverse impacts on profits or share prices.

Another reason for the revival of interest in adverse publicity as a sanction against corporations has been a mounting dissatisfaction with the punitive capacity of fines or monetary penalties. Thus, in a recent case of toxic waste dumping in Los Angeles, the defendant corporation was ordered to advertise its crime in The Wall Street Journal. In the opinion of the judge imposing sentence, deterrence required a punishment that could not be regarded as "just another cost of doing business."

An interesting philosophical basis for using publicity as a sanction has recently been advanced by Peter French. At present, French argues, criminal law reflects a guilt-based system of morality and such an approach is objectionable on many grounds. A shame-based morality is more commendable because it stresses forward-looking exemplary models of behavior rather than retrogressive introspection, but this and other features of a shame-based approach have been relatively neglected in the past.

In French's view, the sanction of publicity is necessary if shame is to be used effectively as a means of social control. Essentially, shame is seen as a visual concept and one dependent on a sensibility to oneself. An adept penal system, it is maintained, is one that can induce shame when there has been a notable incongruity with accepted models of behavior, and uses the visual and media capabilities society to bring out the incongruity and to channel the offender's behavior in an exemplary direction.

In what respects might punitive publicity sanctions help to overcome the previously-described limitations of fines or monetary penalties?

First, publicity orders could be used without falling into the deterrent and retribution traps which exist where a company has committed a serious offense but lacks sufficient liquidity to pay a fine in an appropriate large amount. Second, publicity orders would be directed primarily toward the infliction of loss of corporate prestige, and hence would achieve congruence with this important non-financial value in organizational decision making. Third, adverse publicity orders would provide a sanction unique well-equipped to express the socially-unwanted nature of serious corporate offenses. The potential in this regard is well illustrated by the publicity recently imposed on American Caster Corporation for unlawful toxic was disposal. The advertisement which the company was required to place the Los Angeles Times bore the heading "WARNING" and read partly follows:

Pollution of our environment has become a crisis. Intentional clandestine acts of illegal disposal of hazardous waste, or "midnight dumping" are violent crimes against the community.

Fourth, adverse publicity orders against corporate defendants would not necessarily be exclusively corporate in orientation but, with the aid of probation, could also help to promote individual accountability. As Coffee has suggested there is a valuable hint to be taken from the McCloy report documenting Gulf Oil's bribery practices. The report, prepared by an outside counsel in response to SEC enforcement initiatives, not only trigger, substantial procedural reforms but also hastened the resignation of officials named in it. Furthermore, the revelations in the report were such as receive the attention of the press, and the report itself became a paperback bestseller. Taking this example as a starting-point, Coffee has proposed that corporate offenders be required to employ outside counsel to prepare a compliance report which names the key personnel involved and outlines in readable form what they did. Probationary pre-sentence reports would mandatorily be prepared in considerable factual depth in the expectation that such studies will either find an audience in their own right or, more typically, provide the database for investigative journalism.

Fifth, although adverse publicity orders would not guarantee reform of procedures or policies likely to result in a corporation re-offending, they could be used in such a way as to put public pressure on a defendant to move in that direction. Thus, it would be possible when framing a publicity order to pay explicit attention to the nature of the steps, if any, taken by a corporation to undertake institutional changes after the commission of an offense.

Sixth, adverse publicity orders could be designed to inflict loss of prestige primarily on managers and thereby to reduce overspills to workers and consumers. It may be argued in response that, even if adverse publicity were used primarily for the purpose of inflicting loss of prestige, unacceptable overspills through loss of sales would still result. However, this is not likely to be a significant problem except in the context of offenses relating to dangerous products, and in that context one has to weigh up the relative interests of workers, on the one hand, and consumer victims, on the other.

Finally as regards potential advantages, adverse publicity could be useful where a local subsidiary of a multinational company is sentenced. As we have seen, the practical limit of a fine is governed by the amount of the subsidiary's assets and the extent to which those assets can be seized without crucifying local workers and trade creditors. A publicity sanction, by contrast, is not subject to these constraints because monetary loss is not the object of sentence; what matters is the corporate defendant's reputation. And once the focus shifts to reputation it is possible to transcend jurisdictional borders. Thus, the reputation of a subsidiary like Browning Arms Canada cannot be divorced from that of a parent company like Browning Arms U.S.; both stem from identical organizational roots. A publicity sanction of appropriate design would therefore be aimed not only at the local populace but also at the transnational range of people whose attitudes influence and govern the Browning Arms image in Canada; advertisements would need to be placed in leading U.S. and European media (selectively, so as to keep costs within reasonable bounds) as well as in local outlets.

One objection to the introduction of adverse publicity as a formal sanction against corporations is that the impact of publicity would be uncertain in impact whereas the quantum of cash or equity fines is fixed at a finite amount. Superficially plausible as this objection may be, it seems unpersuasive. To begin with, the comparison should relate to the actual impact of sanctions, not their formally quantified level. Sentences of adverse publicity (or probation, or community service) could also be imposed in terms of some formally quantified level of expenditure. This being so, it must be wondered whether the actual impact of fines or monetary penalties on corporations is any more predictable than the actual impact of adverse publicity (or probation, or community service). For example, when executives at Ford it Detroit were interviewed about the impact of a $7 million environmental fine imposed on their corporation in 1973, the answer was that, in a period when the demand for their cars was strong, the impact was minimal. But fortunes change quickly in the auto industry, and the impact of such a fine in the late 1970s or early 1980s would have been utterly different. Beyond examples such as this, the point has already been made that, although fines or monetary penalties are supposed in theory to catalyze internal discipline or organizational reform, the actual impact may easily be confined to payment of the monetary demand imposed.

Community service

Community service has been required as a condition of corporate probation or non-prosecution in several cases. In the two best-known instances, Unite States v. Allied Chemical Corporation and United States v. Olin Mathieson payment of money for charitable purposes was involved (in the former case to establish the Virginia Environmental Endowment; in the latter, to set up the New Haven Betterment Fund). Likewise, in a more recent case when a highway construction company was convicted of fraudulent tendering for highway contracts, the defendant was required to donate $1.5 million to endow a professorship in ethics at the University of Nebraska. This approach to sentencing, like that of imposing fines or monetary penalties, merely requires the defendant to write a check and, unlike the position in the case of fines or monetary penalties, gives the defendant a public relations bonus.

By contrast, in United States v Danilow Pastry Co., six bakeries convicted of price-fixing were fined with substantial parts of the fines being suspended on the condition that the bakeries provide 12 months' free supplies of fresh baked goods to various needy organizations in the New York area. In imposing this sentence, the court emphasized two factors. First, fines commensurate with the gravity of the offenses would bankrupt the defendants and send them out of business; and second, substituted payment by means of free supply of products to welfare organizations would require the defendants to make "symbolic restitution" for their offenses by doing something more exacting and thought-provoking than handing over money.

Community service orders would offer several potential advantages over fines or monetary penalties.

First, a sentence of personally-performed community service need not slip into the deterrence or retribution trap of limited corporate financial liquidity. Consider the position of the Distillers Company in the thalidomide tragedy. If, for argument's sake, the company had been convicted of a serious offense. Short of bankrupting a company in this predicament, it would be possible to subject it to a community service order requiring it to relieve the plight of victims. One suitable project would be to set up and administer a development and manufacturing facility to produce and supply artificial limbs, robotic devices, and other special aids which, by reason of their limited market, would not otherwise be produced by private enterprise. Were the court to require the company to continue the project over the lifetime of the thalidomide victims, whose needs would alter as they grew and their handicaps changed, the sentence would be serious in terms of both duration and cumulative impact, yet the immediate or annual cost to the company could be fixed at a level unlikely to cripple it.

Second, community service orders would offer a means of impinging upon non-financial as well as financial motivations. Whereas cash fines or penalties require only the payment of money, personally-performed community service would require the expenditure of time and effort.

Third, by requiring the expenditure of time and effort, community-set vice orders would help to project the unwanted corporate offense Whereas fines convey the impression that crime is open to those prepare to pay a tariff this form of sanction would tag such conduct "not for sale.'

Fourth, as far as promoting individual accountability is concerned, community service orders might help to stimulate internal discipline. In being forced to allocate personnel to a project of community service, corporate defendants might be encouraged to ask those persons responsible for getting the company into trouble to perform the necessary acts of rescue.

Fifth, there would also be some advantage in relation to the problem of overspills. Community service projects could create new employment opportunities for persons unemployed or at risk of being laid off. Although the projects would impose financial costs, and although these costs might be passed on to consumers, there would at least be a positive externality namely the service rendered to the community.

The major limitation is that most kinds of community service order would lack the ability to provide any guarantee of adequate organizational reform after the commission of an offense. An exception to this would be a combined sentence of community service and probation requiring a defendant to develop innovative compliance controls and to prepare instructions and follow-up reports with a view to their use by other corporations as a freely available guide.

The prospect of community service as a sanction against corporations raises two obvious concerns: first, the opportunity for judges to channel corporate resources into pet charity programs or frolicsome ventures; and second, and the risk of corporate cheating. These potential sources of trouble however, might be managed by appropriately design or management of the sanction.

Capricious judicial allocation of resources could be kept in check by requiring that the community service projects bear a reasonable relationship either to the offense subject to sentence or to the offender's potential for rehabilitation. Alternatively, the problem could be avoided by requiring that the community service project be selected from a range of projects authorized by statute or delegated legislation.

Less tractable is the risk of corporate cheating by falsifying compliance reports, recycling projects already completed in the normal course of business, or enlisting second or third rate personnel for the project. Yet even this minus danger might be curtailed by a well-designed set of safeguards. The possibilities include provision for court-appointed monitors, requirements that defendants bear the costs when there is a need to escalate supervision or independent verification, and an incentive in the form of recording no conviction when a defendant undertakes an exemplary project of community service.

Conclusion on additional sanctions against corporations

Fines and monetary penalties are now used extensively as sanctions against corporations, but stock dilution (equity fines), probation and punitive injunctions, publicity orders, and community service also merit consideration additional sentencing options. These alternatives seem promising because increasing the variety of deterrent, retributive and rehabilitative impacts achievable against corporations, they offer ways of angling around the major imitations of monetary sanctions. This is not to suggest that fines or monetary penalties have no useful role to play. In many instances, especially less serious offenses, fines are often an expedient and adequate solution. Nor is it suggested that any one alternative represents some ideal type of sanction against corporations. The anatomy of corporate crime is so diverse that effective sentencing requires courts and tribunals to be equipped with a range of available sanctions, not merely one.

Numerous points of detail need to be settled and cast in suitable legislative form, but this should not distract attention from the need for sanctions which are capable of pressing upon the nerves of corporate decision making and thereby giving the law more chance of achieving deterrence, retribution, and rehabilitation.

The objection undoubtedly will be raised that it is unjust to subject corporations to more severe forms of punishment (especially adverse publicity and punitive injunctions) when there is no satisfactory legal concept of corporate fault; unlike the position in the case of individual offenders, the lay has failed to develop any workable concept of corporate blameworthiness. This is a large issue but two brief responses may suffice here. First, there is an increasing body of empirical evidence to the effect that enforcement agencies in the corporate arena lack both the resources and the willingness to prosecute except in extreme cases, notably those involving flagrant violation or persistent non-compliance despite warning. Second, looking ahead it is conceivable that a workable concept of corporate fault could be devise, and several detailed proposals have been made to that end.

Economic efficiency and inegalitarianism

The canon of economic efficiency, if used as the foundation for devising and applying sanctions against corporations, has several anti-egalitarian tendencies. First, the kind of sanction contemplated—monetary exaction—is extraordinarily benign as compared with imprisonment, the archetypal sanction deployed against serious traditional forms of crime. Second, economic efficiency seems to herald the compromise of individual accountability for wrongdoing in the corporate sector yet not in the more traditional domain of criminal law.

Benign discrimination in punishment

A recurrent theme in the literature on corporate crime is the disparity between the severity of sentences handed out to small-time individual offender and the relative leniency of the sentences typically imposed on big-time corporate offenders. Economically efficient monetary punishment, if it could be applied to individual as well as to corporate offenders, would help to avoid this inegalitarian bias but there is little chance of this happening.

Pleas have often been made for reduction of the severity of punishment of street crime so as to achieve a more even-handed deal in the treatment of corporate and individual offenders. Speaking of the position in Great0Britain, Steven Box has recently made the following observation:

> Maybe such considerations will ... mellow our attitude towards the imprisonment of nearly 9,000 men and 500 women (representing nearly 25 and 45 per cent respectively of all those sentenced to immediate imprisonment) for theft, handling stolen goods, fraud, and forgery, when the amounts of value involved are nothing in comparison with the millions stolen by offending corporations on whom our criminal justice system has given up. If there is no way of implementing justice for the largest and worst offending corporations then it is surely unjust to pursue with such ruthless and cruel tenacity the majority of those eventually condemned to prison.

Perhaps such a mellowing in attitude might come to pass if economic efficiency were to reign in the sphere of such offenses as theft, handling stolen goods, fraud, and forgery but there seems little prospect of this occurring. Few offenders have the ability to pay fines in the amount needed to reflect the conventionally perceived gravity of these offenses against property and reliance the reliance on jail and other non-monetary forms of punishment. It has been urged that the inability of some offenders to pay fines is no reason Or denying that opportunity to those who do have the resources to pay, but this raises quite starkly the ethical hazard of having one law for the rich and another for the poor.

Compromise of individual accountability for wrongdoing in the corporate sector

Another inegalitarian bias of economic efficiency as a policy foundation for the design and application of sanctions lies in the apparent lack of importance attached to individual accountability. Individual accountability is given little apparent weight as a means of controlling corporate wrongdoing whereas individual accountability is insisted upon in the social control of street crime.

The seat of the problem here is the assumption in mainstream economics that a company is a rational actor akin to Stanley Jevons' "economic man" This conception of organizational decision making is unrealistic, as John Byrne and Steven Hoffman have explained:

> The most visible difficulty in using this modified nineteenth century model to describe contemporary corporate criminal decision making is that it was constructed to stand for the thought patterns and behavior of an individual, not the twentieth century corporation composed of many individuals, ... products, ... decisions, many values, and many goals. Economists for the most part, however, have been unconvinced that this obvious disjuncture between theory and reality requires significant repair of their ideas about firm decision making.

One consequence of allegiance to the rational actor model in economically efficient approaches to sanctioning corporations is that the distinction between individual and corporate accountability is either blurred or disregarded in favor of treating the corporation as the only rational actor to be held responsible. It might also be contended that individual accountability is not as efficient as corporate accountability (partly because the latter serves as a fast and cheap one-stop operation for enforcers, and partly because corporate enforcement systems provide an expeditious way of locating individual accountability within an organization) and hence is relatively unimportant. Certainly, the leading proponents of economically efficient sanctions again: corporations do not stress the value of individual accountability. Moreover as has been pointed out earlier, fines or monetary penalties against a company provide no guarantee that the company will react by taking internal disciplinary action against personnel implicated in the relevant wrongdoing Only if the law were to enter the black box of a company (e. g. by means probation or a punitive injunction) would the punishment of the company result in any legal obligation to pursue the matter of individual accountability.

To the extent that individual accountability seemingly drops out of the equation if sanctions against corporate wrongdoing are governed by the calculus of economic efficiency, there is reason to wonder about the equity the degree of immunity that would thereby be conferred on individuals who committed offenses on behalf of corporations. It has been observed till in the West decision making is presented as individualistic until adversity proves it collective. A policy of economic efficiency, it would seem, might embrace this cynical habit and have it enshrined in corporate regulation. By contrast, individual offenders outside the corporate sector would not have a corporate rational actor to shield them and hence could not enjoy the same relief from personal accountability for wrongdoing.

Conclusion on economic efficiency and inegalitarianism

As a foundation for the design and application of sanctions against corpora-ions, the canon of economic efficiency has inegalitarian tendencies. Beyond he concerns expressed above, there is a risk that economic efficiency might be politically manipulated so as surreptitiously to promote an inequitable approach to the control of corporate wrongdoing.

Many examples can be found of legislation which has been introduced in seeming attempt to exert effective control over corporate wrongdoing yet which in reality has been a token effort. As W.G. Carson has observed in his analysis of the forces which led to the enactment of the Factory Regulation Act, 1833 (U.K.), corporate regulation can actually be welcomed by the regulated where the legislation symbolizes the moral stature of owners of capital and does not threaten to portray them as members of the criminal classes. a light of this experience, the possibility exists that an economically efficient regime of fines or monetary penalties against corporate wrongdoing might be introduced so as politically to create the illusion of effective social control.

An economically efficient regime of fines or monetary penalties would authorize the infliction of very large financial exactions from corporations; recollect the proposal of Elzinga and Breit that antitrust violations should be penalized by a man-datory penalty of 25% of a firm's pre-tax profits for every year of anti-competitive activity. To this extent, the appearance sight easily be created that society had taken a firm hand against corporate wrongdoing. In practice, however, heavy fines would probably be very rare. As we have seen, the ability or willingness of a court to impose a large fine on company is constrained by the financial wealth of the company, and by the risk of causing unwanted overspills to shareholders, workers or consumers. The political platform of economically efficient monetary sanctions against corporations thus holds out the promise that serious corporate offenses will be punished stringently with high fines but masks the inegalitarian reality that courts will find themselves constrained to impose relatively low fines even in serious cases.

Providing additional forms of sanction against corporations— for example, equity fines, probation and punitive injunctions, adverse publicity, and community service—would hardly be enough in itself to ensure that the la treated serious corporate offenses seriously. However, these additional forms of sanction would not be subject to the same kind of political false promise as that of "efficient" fines. As contended earlier, punitive injunctions, one or more of the other possible alternatives canvassed, would usually capable of delivering a stiff punitive impact even where the inability of the company to pay, or the risk of causing unacceptable overspills, precluded the imposition of a heavy fine.

Conclusion

A number of influential attempts have been made to reduce the problem effectively punishing corporate wrongdoing to a quest for economic efficient through the use of fines or monetary penalties. The argument of this papa has been that this approach is unsatisfactory, partly because it neglects the limitations of fines or monetary penalties, and partly because it has troubling inegalitarian tendencies. An alternative approach, commended here, to pin down the reasons why fines and monetary penalties against corporations have been criticized in the past, and to explore the potential of various alternative sanctions for overcoming the weaknesses of monetary punishment. The possibilities explored—equity fines (stock dilution), probation and punitive injunctions, adverse publicity, and community service— seem promising in different ways. Conceivably these possibilities could be developed so as to provide a flexible and potent array of sanctions. If so, we would not necessarily achieve economic efficiency but we might equip the law with punishments to fit major as well as minor corporate crime.

*I would like to thank Graeme Coss for research assistance.

5. Retributivism, punishment and privilege

John Braithwaite*

"Just deserts" as a rationale for punishing criminals means that offenders ought be punished not for the sake of crime prevention, but because they deserve it, for the sake of retribution (e. g. von Hirsch, 1976; Singer, 1979). the quantum of their punishment should be in proportion to the seriousness of their offense, not according to any assessment of whether they are rehabilitated or any estimation of the need for deterrence.

Just deserts has proved an attractive philosophy in part because it is seen by many of its followers as involving no tragic choices. Because the most serious offenses, those deserving most punishment, are also those where the seed for deterrence and incapacitation of dangerous offenders is greatest, the demands of just deserts and protection of the community seem to be in step. At the same time, however, it can be argued that in a large proportion of cases, punishment of known offenders does more harm than good. This can be particularly so with young offenders, for whom prison can be "school for crime" where professional skills in, for example, safe cracking, are imparted, where reference groups are adopted which provide social support for criminality, where resentments can be enhanced by acts of violence and degradation directed against the offender, and where opportunities for earning income legitimately are interrupted. Even without incarceration the labeling that goes with other punishments might enhance criminal self. conceptions (Lemert, 1951; Becker, 1963; West and Farrington, 1977). On balance, most defenders of just deserts are not overly troubled by these arguments. While conceding that they may have some merit, retributivist: tend to be reluctant to believe that there are many cases where imposing the deserved punishment puts the community at greater risk. Mostly, they suspect, the counterproductive effects of imposing deserved punishments are outweighed by the benefits of deterrence and incapacitation.

Just deserts as inconsistent with protecting the community from white-collar crime

In this article, I will argue that with white-collar crime there are some special reasons why punishment can be counterproductive. These pose more starkly the possibility that the lives of citizens are poorly protected by an enforcement policy which puts retribution ahead of prevention. White-collar crime is defined, according to the conventional definition of Sutherland (1949:2) as "a crime committed by a person of respectability and high social status in the course of his [or her] occupation." For the purposes of this article common crime means all crime which is not white-collar.

Blunderbuss punishment and business compliance

A literature is accumulating in the field of business regulatory enforcement which suggests the sensitivity with which punishment must be used as method of social control (Bardach and Kagan, 1982; Braithwaite, 1985 Cranston, 1979; Hawkins, 1984; Shover et al. 1983; Hawkins and Thomas 1984). Business regulatory agencies can sap the will of business to corn ply with the law by remorselessly punishing them whenever they slip up b: breaching health and safety, consumer protection, pollution, antitrust, and other laws.

This is because, at its worst, an uncompromising punitive strategy can lead to what Bardach and Kagan call an "organized culture of resistance"— a culture that facilitates the sharing of knowledge about the methods of legal resistance and counter-attack. As an example, Bardach and Kagan cite the advice of one legal expert to appeal all Occupational Health and Safety Administration (OSHA) citations, not just those to which companies object strongly, so that they can "settle a case by giving up on some items in exchange for dismissal by OSHA of others. Those who leave certain things uncontested are needlessly giving up this possibility" (1983: 114).

Dissipating the motivation of business to strive for compliance with the law is a disastrous consequence because the punitive law enforcement alternative can never fill the gaps left by the failure of persuasion and education as compliance strategies. With all complex areas of business regulation one can never write rules to protect people against all the unsafe or exploitative practices that can occur. Since building consensus to write new rules is a difficult and time-consuming process, since rule writing does not keep up with rapidly changing technology, and since every business poses unique problems, government regulations never cover the field. The British, who have achieved the safest coal mines in the world, make the point that, if their inspectors enforced strict compliance with the Mines and Quarries Act L954 and the regulations arising there from, they would enforce a far lower standard of safety practice than they in fact do. It is persuasion, heeded by responsible managers, which achieves the higher standards.

Achieving better than the minimum standards set down in law is imperative, but inspectors will not succeed if punishment has been used with so little finesse that they lose their capacity to persuade. Perhaps one reason that the United States has such a shocking coal mine fatality rate is that trust and respect between inspectors and managers has been lost by blunderbuss punishment policies. As the chief executive of the Bituminous Coal Operators' Association said when I interviewed him in 1982:

> Lives are lost because of inspectors with the paper syndrome and companies with the "How do we minimize the violations?" syndrome.

Government inspectors achieve more by adopting a diagnostic and catalytic role than they can by focusing excessively on punishment. Bardach and Kagan underlined this point by quoting the safety director of a large corporation on what he thought OSHA inspectors should do:

> OSHA inspectors have the right to talk to employees. They'll go up to a machine operator and ask if everything is OK. What they really mean is, "Is there a violation I can write up?" If the man points out a broken electrical cord or plug, the OSHA guy will just write it up and put it on the list of citations.

What they should do is this: He should ask the employee, "How long has it been that way? Did you tell your foreman about it?" He should call over the foreman and ask why it was still that way. Maybe the foreman will say, "I've told him three times ... you're supposed to go to Supply and get a new cord." Then why didn't he? Maybe his job is set up so he can't. Maybe the inspector will find out there's no procedure for checking cords, or that there is, but that the employees don't know it well (1982:1489).

What the offender deserves or what the victim deserves?

For white-collar crimes against the person—the very crimes about which the data show greatest community punitiveness—the case for selective enforcement is strongest. This is because the offense so often poses a continuing danger to the community. "Just deserts" must at times be sacrificed for protection of the public. Regulatory agencies often resist the urge to prosecute guilty parties when the cooperation of those parties is needed to safeguard the public health. If a drug company has criminally negligent quality control procedures which are putting the community at risk, an injunction to close down the plant followed by a criminal prosecution can set company lawyers to work on very effective delaying tactics (Braithwaite, 1984). Justice delayed is profits retained. The public interest will often be better served by an approach to the company offering immunity from prosecution if it will cooperate in a package of measures which might include a voluntary recall of certain batches of impure drugs from the market, dismissal of certain irresponsible quality control staff, revision of standard operating procedures t(improve product quality, and compensation to victims of the impure drugs In a haphazard fashion, such negotiated settlements foster deterrence, often more so than a paltry fine which might be handed down by a court. But more importantly, they do so while minimizing the risk to consumers. The voluntary recall of drugs already on the market is almost invariably more rapid and efficient (in the sense of maximizing the proportion of the batch which is located) than a court-ordered seizure (Hutt, 1973). Only the company knows where all of its product has gone. A seizure which is resisted by the company faces considerable practical difficulties.

A classic illustration of the dilemmas in choosing between retribution against alleged white-collar criminals and the wider public interest was the aftermath of the thalidomide drug disaster (Knightley et al. , 1979: 122-36). Nine executives of Chemie Grunenthal, the manufacturer of thalidomide, were indicted in Germany on charges of intent to commit bodily harm and involuntary manslaughter. After the complex legal proceedings had dragged a for five years, including over two years in court, the charges were dropped as part of a deal in which Grunenthal agreed to pay $31 million in compensation to the German thalidomide children. The press cried "justice for sale." But the German government had to consider the ongoing misery of the thalidomide families who up to that point had struggled for nine years rearing their deformed and limbless children without any financial assistance. Would retribution against Grunenthal and its executives have justified perhaps another nine years of waiting and deprivation for the victims?

Learning to prevent crime by withholding punishment

There are many reasons for not prosecuting even some violations which endanger human life. It is usually not good inspectorial practice to recommend prosecution when the company comes forward and admits a violation. Thus, for example, airlines must be encouraged to report near disasters, however culpable they may be in relation to them, so that real disasters can be prevented not only with the airline concerned, but for all others around the world. It would be the height of irresponsibility to allow policy in relation to such matters to be driven by considerations of retribution rather than protection of the community.

Informal social control—the only affordable policy?

Although there are many more compelling reasons for not consistently prosecuting white-collar offenders, cost is undoubtedly the most influential reason in practice. Philip Schrag's (1971) gripping account of what happened when he took over the enforcement division of the New York City Department of Consumer Affairs underlines the inevitability of a retreat from commit-lent to consistent and equitable enforcement of the law when dealing with white-collar crime. When Schrag began in the job he adopted a prosecutorial stance. In response, however, to a variety of frustrations, especially the use of delaying tactics by company lawyers, a "direct action" model was eventually substituted for the "judicial" model. Non-litigious methods of thieving restitution, deterrence, and incapacitation were increasingly used. These included threats and use of adverse publicity, revocation of license, writing directly to consumers to warn them of company practices, and exerting pressure on reputable financial institutions and suppliers to withdraw support for the targeted company.

Whether we approve of the retreat from the justice model with white collar crime, it must be conceded that, given the legal system we have inherited, the public gets most of its protection from extra-legal muscle-flexing by regulators which persuades companies to change their ways. We might shudder at the cavalier disregard of due process by the inspector who says, "fix that up or I'll be back once a month looking for things to nab you on." But to the extent that white-collar crime is prevented in modern societies such muscle-flexing is the most important way it happens. Moreover, I suspect that most companies would prefer to live with a little of such coercion every now and then than with the legal costs of a more litigious relationship with government agencies.

Consistent administration of justice becomes impossible in the face or the costs of litigating complex white-collar cases. Prosecutors must confront complexity in the accounts (Briloff, 1972; Sutton and Wild, 1979), complexity of the law (Sutton and Wild, 1978), complexity of organizational real ties (Stone, 1975; Ermann and Lundman, 1978; Schrager and Short, 1978) complexity of scientific dispute (Braithwaite, 1984), and jurisdictional complexities in crimes which transcend national boundaries (Blum, 1984). Many types of complexity are exploited by the talented counsel which white-collar defendants can usually afford to retain, and also by the defendants then selves. For example, books of account are confusing because the white-collar criminal wants them that way. A potentially simple transaction is intentionally concealed by a round robin or daisy chain arrangement through series of intermediary transactions. The inherent and contrived complexity of white-collar crime makes proof of guilt beyond reasonable doubt an onerous burden indeed.

At the same time, most regulatory agencies are cognizant of the need for a degree of formal and public punishment to maintain the habit-forming value of law and to foster deterrence. These ends can be achieved by high' selective white-collar crime enforcement policies in which only occasion, offenders are made an example of. The offenders chosen are usually those for whom none of the aforementioned arguments against prosecution apply. They are chosen not because they are the most deserving of punishment, but because their case would be less costly than others, because their cooperation is not required to retrieve dangerous drugs from the market, and so on.

Summary

In summary, two things are being suggested. First, to allow retribution to take precedence over protection of the community in regulating businesses such as airlines, food and drug manufacture, coal mining, and many others, is to make justice a more important societal goal than protection of human life. Second, the reality of enforcing the law against business violations which are vast in number, complex in nature, and formidably defended, is that there is no society, and never will be a society, that will allow the dispensation of deserved punishment to be the principle which guides efforts to secure business compliance with the law. A just deserts model of business regulatory enforcement is neither desirable nor remotely obtainable in practice.

Just deserts for the poor, gentle persuasion for the rich?

For the just deserts theorist who is moved by the argument thus far, we now consider the solution of rejecting just deserts as a principle to guide business regulatory enforcement and retaining it with enforcement against common crime. It will be concluded that this is a morally untenable choice, because, if one believes in desert, it is with white-collar crime where desert is greatest.

The difference between white-collar crime enforcement against business and enforcement against common crime is that, whatever one thinks of the desirability of just deserts with common crime, it is certainly attainable in practice in a way that it is not with white-collar crime. While there is no business regulatory bureaucracy in the world which gives higher priority to desert than to prevention, there are many bureaucracies for dealing with common crime which have the dispensation of deserved punishment as their primary goal. In my own research on business regulatory agencies, I have studied over 100 agencies on four continents without discovering one for which just deserts was a significant priority or even a subsidiary goal. The day the literature reports a regulatory agency driven by desert, it will be akin to a zoologist announcing the discovery of a new species.

Just deserts is a feasible principle for organizing bureaucracies which deal with common crime; it is infeasible for business crime. What is wrong then with a society which allows desert to be the principle which guides common criminal law, while protection of the community guides food and drug, antitrust and similar laws? Pandemic class injustice is what's wrong. Such a position means that it is acceptable to fail to give deserved punishment to known ruling class criminals, but unacceptable for known common criminals. Just deserts would then be a rationalization for ruling class justice. An escape route from this dilemma for defenders of desert is to assert that business offenders do not often deserve to be punished because an offense against say the environment is not a "real" crime, that business offenses rarely tend to be so serious as to deserve punishment.

White-collar crime as "deserving" of more punishment than common crime

I have reviewed evidence relevant to the foregoing escape route at length elsewhere. First, if the legislature determines that a business regulatory offense is a crime, it is hard for retributivists who believe in the legitimacy of the legislature to make such determinations to suggest that they did not know what they were doing or that they did not intend them to be "real crimes."

Second, if objective harm (property lost, numbers of persons seriously injured or killed) is a central determinant of desert, as most retributivists insist, I have shown that the evidence is overwhelming that business offenses cause much more objective harm than common crimes (Braithwaite, 1982e 742-7). Sutherland (1949: 121-22) was the first to collect together sufficient white-collar crimes to show that "the financial cost of white-collar crime is probably several times as great as the financial cost of all the crimes which are customarily regarded as the 'crime problem'," though at the end of the last century Barrett (1895) showed that banks lost more from fraud and embezzlement than from bank robberies. Similarly, if one counts up the lives lost through offenses against consumer product safety, occupations health and safety and environmental laws, even in a society with a homicide rate as extraordinary as the United States, it is the former which cost more lives.

Third, I have shown from a review of a large number of public opinion surveys that if community perceptions of the seriousness of different crime are the criterion of desert, then white-collar crimes deserve massively more severe punishment than they are receiving at the moment:

> ...the community perceives many forms of white-collar crime as more serious, and deserving of more severe punishment, than most forms of common crime. There are exceptions to this pattern. Tax offenses and false advertising in most studies are not viewed as serious crimes. Most types of individual homicide are perceived as more serious than all types of white-collar crime. Nevertheless, white-collar crimes which cause severe harm to persons are generally rated as more serious than all other types

of crime and even some types of individual homicide (Braithwaite, 1982a: 738).

Fourth, I have shown that, if we exclude traffic or victimless offenses, the sheer volume of white-collar crime is so enormous as to vastly outnumber common offenses in the community (Braithwaite, 1982a: 745-7). To use one minor illustration, the Mine Safety and Health Administration imposes fines for some 140,000 corporate coal mine safety violations every year.

Admittedly, many of these offenses are not intentional, and therefore lack the mens rea which is the hallmark of serious crime. But many are—so many that I concluded in the earlier review that:

> ... among that subset of crime which is intentional, white-collar crimes are greater in number and in harm (measured either objectively [dollars or lives lost] or subjectively [community ratings of seriousness or deserved punishment]). Therefore, it is reasonable to assert that just deserts, whether based on a subjective or objective calculus, implies that there should be more white-collar criminals sent to prison than common criminals. (Braithwaite, 1982a: 750)

Where desert is greatest, punishment will be least

We have seen that transforming our prisons to primarily custodians of white-collar offenders is neither desirable nor possible, notwithstanding the fact that this is implied by policies systematically to operationalize community perceptions of desert. When an agency like California OSHA prosecuted And fined only 5 of over 200,000 offenses detected in one year (Mendeloff, 1979: 83-85), we can certainly say this is not enough to achieve deterrence, but to say that all of these offenses which the community believes are deserving of severe punishment should be so punished, or all of those offenses which involve both mens rea and objective harm should be punished in proportion to the harm, is to advocate a redeployment of criminal justice resources of unimaginable proportions. It can and should never happen. And similarly, with other areas of white-collar crime enforcement. As Norval Morris says of tax violations: "Not every tax felon need be imprisoned, only a number sufficient to keep the law's promises and to encourage the rest of us to honest in our tax returns." (Morris, 1974:9).

Even though we can and should do much to step up prosecutions of white-collar criminals, it will always be the case that only a tiny fraction of white-collar criminals will ever be prosecuted even after they become suspects. Paradoxically, the arguments for doing deals which include immunity from prosecution are typically most compelling in those types of cases which the public see as most deserving of punishment (crimes which threaten the lives of consumers). Second, the bigger the case, the more likely that it will be so complex as to render the costs of prosecution prohibitive. Third, the more ruthless and powerful the criminal, the greater the willingness and the capacity consciously to contrive complexity into the case. All this is part or a more general theorem of criminal justice: Where desert is greatest, punishment will be least. Empirical work on system capacity with respect to common crime suggests that those locations where crime is most widespread and serious are precisely the locations where the system resorts to leniency in order to keep cases moving and avert system overload (Pontell, 1978). In the rare cases where individual white-collar criminals are brought to justice systematic forces make it unlikely that these will be the most blameworthy individuals. Whether they are junior scapegoats, or middle management "vice-presidents responsible for going to jail" such as some pharmaceutics companies have institutionalized to protect top management, these systematic forces push blame for white-collar crime downwards in the class structure (Braithwaite, 1982b).

It has been argued here that if just deserts were to work in practice, there would be many more white-collar criminals in prison than common criminals. Putting aside all the other factors which make this impossible, cost alone would prevent any government from processing all the complex case which would be required to make the majority of our prisoners white-collar criminals. It is not simply that no matter how hard we try consistently to administer just deserts, we can only ever imperfectly achieve the goal. Rather, identifiable structural reasons will cause any attempt to administer just deserts to produce precisely the opposite effect: the locations in space time, and in the class structure where desert is least become the location where punishment is greatest. Just deserts can be implemented in a rough and ready way against common criminals; it cannot begin to be implemented against white-collar criminals. Desert is applied more or less successfully against the poor and unsuccessfully against the rich. Retributivism is therefore a philosophical theory which "may be formally correct (i.e., coherent, or true for some possible world) but materially incorrect (i.e., inapplicable to the actual world in which we live)." (Murphy, 1979: 103).

The alternative?

The solution, it seems to me, is to give up on the quest to impose desert evenhandedly wherever it falls in the class structure. Instead, we should begin to think about how to apply the principle of parsimony even-handedly (Morris, 1974: 60-61). This principle tells us that we should resort to punishment only when there is no more constructive way of solving a social problem. It follows that in the face of limited evidence that deterrence (Beyleveld, 1980), incapacitation (Van Dine et al., 1979) and rehabilitation (Lipton, Martinson and Wilks, 1975) actually work in protecting the community from common crime, and we should let most common criminals out of prison. One challenge for a unified consequentialist theory of criminal justice is to specify when to use what alternative remedies with the decarcerated. In collaboration with Philip Pettit, I intend to detail such a theory in a future publication.

While most white-collar crimes should also continue to be unpunished on grounds of parsimony, there is reason to believe that we are not solving problems such as occupational disease and pollution partly because of insufficient punishment (e. g. Clinard and Yeager, 1980; Braithwaite, 1985). The principle of parsimony gives us the latitude to move toward class justice by simultaneously decreasing the punishment of common criminals and increasing that of white-collar criminals.

Just deserts, in contrast, only gives us the option of imposing desert successfully against the poor and unsuccessfully against the rich. The irony is that under just deserts—the philosophy of punishment which sets out with justice as its primary goal—justice is sociologically impossible.

*Thanks to Philip Pettit for perceptive criticisms of an earlier draft of this chapter.

6. Punishment, privilege and structured choice

W. Byron Groves and Nancy Frank

In the previous chapter, John Braithwaite offered a rather disturbing formula for punishment. The formula was: where desert is greatest, punishment will be least. The reference was to white-collar criminals, and the implication was that once we take into consideration the relative seriousness of their offenses, persons convicted of these crimes deserve more punishment than they receive.

The intent of the present article is to reinforce this point, and central to our argument will be (1) an analysis of the extent to which social class determines patterns of criminality, and (2) the implications this has for issues such as freedom and moral responsibility. We wish to supplement Braithwaite's formula by amending it to read: among those who commit crimes, punishment will be greatest where it is deserved the least.

The theme for this formula is also implied in a passage taken from one of today's leading advocates of retributivism, Andrew von Hirsch. Towards the end of his very popular book entitled *Doing Justice*, von Hirsch (1976: 78) notes that:

> ...the impoverished defendant poses a dilemma for our (retributive) theory. In principle, a case can be made that he is less culpable because his deprived status has left him with far fewer opportunities for an adequate livelihood within the law.

With certain qualifications, this is exactly the case we shall make in the pages that follow.

Arguments supporting the view that deprivation and diminished opportunities are relevant to considerations of criminal responsibility will be presented in three sections. First, evidence will be reviewed which suggests that social class determines the life chances available to persons at different locations in the stratification hierarchy. Section two will argue that life chance: also influence the type and quality of choices available to persons, making those with abundant life choices "freer" than those whose range of choices is restricted. And finally, we conclude by suggesting that when persons enjoy fewer life choices, there is a greater likelihood that they will commit the kinds of crimes most frequently and severely punished in our society.

In developing this argument, we shall also criticize the legal view of freedom and responsibility, which generally defines both in either/or terms (i.e. either one is free or not free, responsible or not responsible). Having established that choice is structured, and that our legal system ignores this fact by treating all but the insane as equally responsible, we offer a modest suggestion for sentencing reform.

Life Chances and Social Class

It is of the essence of social class that it can create differences in reward where none exist in talent, that it can impose differences in punishment where none exists in obedience to rules. (Travis Hirschi, 1969: 82)

As a foundation for our argument, it is important to demonstrate empirically the ways in which social stratification (i.e., inequality) operates to define the "life chances" of persons located at different positions in the clan structure. The idea is to illustrate ways in which inequality increasingly narrows the range of effective choices open to individuals at lower stations in the stratification hierarchy.

What is the relationship between a person's class position and the type of life chances he or she might enjoy? For some sociologists the best way to define social class is in terms of the number of available life chances. For his part Weber (1977: 181) argues that:

> …it is a most elemental fact that the way in which the disposition over material property is distributed among a plurality of people, meeting competitively in the market for the purpose of exchange, in itself creates specific life chances.

That is to say, class location is a by-product of market relationships. Put in somewhat different terms, Weber is suggesting that one's location in the class structure is not a function of choice, but rather is a function of institutional forces which, for the most part, lie beyond the pale of an individual's ability to manipulate "the system." If the contrary were true, that is, if it could be shown that persons in the lower class are poor because they chose to be lazy or unambitious, we would be hard pressed to make a diminished responsibility argument for those criminal behaviors which are part and parcel of a chosen lower-class lifestyle. To make sense of this let us take drunk driving as an example.

When apprehended for drunk driving we are held responsible for our actions, although at the time of the offense our mental capacity is literally washed away. The reason we are still responsible is that we chose to get trunk, even though we were well aware of the intoxicating effects of alcohol. If poverty too was a matter of choice, the same logic might apply to people who chose poverty, and presumably chose the criminal behaviors which have long been associated with it. By and large, however, empirical research does not support this view.

Reviewing data from the 1950s, C. Wright Mills (1963: 96) saw what he called a master trend emerging in the economic structure which, he claimed, all available data supported. That trend suggested that "the occupational structure is becoming more rigid and, statistically speaking, it is more difficult for the bright young man born into relatively low circumstances to climb above the position occupied by his father." Mills (1963: 121) embellished this claim with the rather depressing observation that "the best statistical chance of becoming a member of the business elite is to be born into it." Do these observations apply today? To answer this question, we briefly summarize some current data on occupational rank, the most commonly used index of inequality in contemporary social mobility research (van Fossen, 1979).

In 1967, Blau and Duncan published their findings on data secured of the lifetime occupational mobility of a representative sample of about 20,000 men between the ages of 20 and 64. Their data show that while there is great deal of mobility in the United States, the bulk of it covers a very short distance. Adding race to their analysis, Blau and Duncan (1967) found that non-whites were more likely to be downwardly mobile and less likely to be upwardly mobile than their white counterparts. In a recent and exhaustive review of available empirical evidence, van Fossen (1979: 201) combines the findings of Mills (1963) and Blau and Duncan (1967) and concludes that for the person who wants to get ahead, "it helps to be born to high status parents [and] to belong to a privileged race."

Numerous other studies (Gilbert and Kahl, 1982; Domhoff, 1967; Feagin 1975; Miller and Roby, 1970; Dahrendorf, 1979) support the claim that one's class position is socially determined and go on to list some of the specific ways in which social class influences an individual's life chances. Making explicit this link between class situation and life chances, Weber (1977:181 argues that:

> we may speak of a 'class' when (1) a number of people have in common a specific causal component of their life chances, insofar as (2) this component is represented exclusively by economic interests in the possession of goods and opportunities for income, and (3) is represented under the conditions of the commodity or labor markets.

Thus, life chances are defined relative to one's class situation, and in a more compact definition Weber refers to classes as "groups of people who share common life opportunities." (Weber in Krisberg, 1975: 22).

Life chances and life opportunities are big terms. Subsumed under they are an assortment of material and psychological variables such as wealth, status, income, power, prestige, honor, self-esteem and lifestyle. In our society living in a class with abundant life chances means, among other things, that one has more money, more wealth, better health care, better education, and more prestigious occupation. As a consequence of these advantages, persons in a privileged social stratum are freed from the daily struggle for basic needs and, hence, are "freer" to develop themselves, to mold their own lives, to take their destiny into their own hands. As Edward Deci (1980) argues, such persons are more likely to achieve freedom via self-determination, and Maslow (1982) has suggested that by freeing themselves from basic needs, well-to-do persons are in a better position to realize higher order needs for self-actualization.

But what of those with diminished life opportunities or life chances? van Fossen (1979: 353) reviews a few of the many consequences suffered by those in lower stations in the class hierarchy:

> In comparison with the American middle and upper classes, the American poor have to deal with lower incomes, inadequate diets, lower levels of physical and mental health, shorter life expectancies, higher birth rates, and economic problems associated with consumption.

Much more could be added to this discussion, particularly with respect t0 the paucity of life chances available to those in the lower social classes. However, enough ground has been covered to make the point that it is a long way from the country club to the ghetto. Ultimately, we shall argue that among the life chances that are crucially influenced by one's social position in modern society is the chance to avoid becoming a criminal or delinquent (Mills, 1963: 309).

To substantiate this claim we move to the second step in our argument. The task is to demonstrate that by limiting the life chances available to certain groups of persons, social class ultimately structures choice. Our assumption is that life is inseparable from the social structure that sets the frontiers to that life, and the bottom line is that, hand in hand with the number and type of available life chances, there comes a proportionate number and type of life choices available to individuals given the logic of their particular class situation.

Two views of freedom and responsibility

[S]ome men are apparently freer than others ... Freedom, like most social qualities, is not randomly distributed. Though each is in some measure constrained, emperor and slave are not equally constrained. Each evades the limits of unfettered freedom and complete constraint, but that should not obscure the great differences between the two. (David Matza, 1964: 8)

Freedom is not an either/or proposition, as certain legal scholars would have us believe. To make this point effectively, we must have a workably definition of freedom squarely before us.

Freedom, as used in this paper, consists of two types of choice: first freedom has to do with the number of choices available to persons give! their social situation, and as such has a quantitative dimension. Simply put the more choices, the more freedom. But this is an insufficient criterion for freedom, and to round out our definition we must add that the available choices must be of a certain quality, i.e., they must be choices that are valued and meaningful within the cultural setting in question. A few examples will make clear why freedom must be discussed in terms of both the number and type of available choices.

Let us imagine a situation where one person has more choices than another but is not "freer" in any meaningful sense of that term. One of two, cellmates is informed that he will be executed by a firing squad in the morning. The other too will be executed but is given the "choice" of being shot or hanged. To be sure, the latter has twice as many choices than the former, but his freedom exists only in the technical or trivial sense that he has more options. Neither he nor his cellmate has a choice relative to the value that really matters in this situation, i.e., the value of life over death. Thus, simple quantitative criterion for freedom, while not wrong, is incomplete.

To see why the type or quality of choices is also important as a criterion for deciding how "free" a person is, let us now contrast the freedom of millionaire with that of a prisoner. For his part, the prisoner is subjected to many constraints and coercive influences which temper his range of choice and eliminate other choices altogether. The prison walls, the guard, the routinization of the day, and a host of other factors exert a deterministic force in the prisoner's life. And yet even under harsh conditions such as these the prisoner is not totally constrained. While in his cell he may choose to stand up or walk a short distance, and even when strapped in a straightjacket h can blink or urinate should he choose to do so.

The millionaire, on the other hand, is considerably less constrained, for he has more choices and more socially valued choices than the prisoner. He may, for instance, decide to have lunch in Paris, or choose to earn prestige by contributing to a hospital. But neither is the millionaire totally free, for his choices too are limited: he cannot be in two places at the same time, nor can he have lunch on Neptune. Nonetheless, as Matza (1964: 8) sensibly notes, while both the prisoner and the millionaire "evade the limits of unfettered freedom and complete constraint that should not obscure the great differences between the two."

In the prisoner/millionaire example it is easy to appreciate the vast differentials that exist in both the number and type of choices available. However, things get complicated when we remove the prisoner from his cell and place him in a ghetto, for now one might argue that the number of choices available to each is roughly equal (e. g., the ghetto dweller cannot lunch in Paris, but neither can the millionaire find street drugs at a moment's notice). But even if we allow the rather dubious assumption that both retain an equal number of choices, the ghetto-dweller is still less free in terms of his ability to acquire socially valued benefits (both material and psychological) such as status, wealth, prestige, honor, property and so on. Thus, by attending to the type as well as the number of available choices, one can reasonably assert that ghetto dwellers are less free than millionaires.

These examples highlight an important point: that freedom is a matter of degree or, put another way, that some are less free than others. While this may seem obvious, the implications of this view have not been adequately addressed by legal scholars. To get an idea of the legal view of the relationship between freedom and responsibility, let us review the position held by philosophers in both the existential tradition and in law as currently practiced in the United States.

The intentions of existentialists are certainly laudable, for one of their goals is to preserve human dignity by rejecting determinism in favor of choice, freedom, and self-determination. For instance, John Paul Sartre takes the example of a prisoner being tortured and argues that, even under this condition of extreme pain and suffering, the prisoner is free because it is he who decides if and when to confess. Perhaps he finds patriotic meaning in suffering (Frankl, 1959), or manages to observe his pain rather than identify with it, as did Solzhenitsyn (1974) in the Gulag. Given these examples, and the fact that some choose not to confess no matter how severe the torture, Sartre's point is not altogether unreasonable.

The existential view is quite provocative, and we would be the last to dismiss it out of hand. However, we believe Sartre overstates his case by arguing for an absolute view of freedom and responsibility. He assumes that we are free so long as we can choose, and because we can make choices in even the most coercive circumstances, Sartre concludes that "man is condemned to be free...[and] is responsible for everything that he does" (Sartre, 1976 393).

Were this view of the relationship between freedom and responsibility confined to existentialists, it could be regarded as interesting philosophical speculation. Unfortunately, it is not so confined. Our legal system mirrors the existential view of freedom by presuming that, so long as persons can choose not to commit a crime, they are responsible for their actions. From this perspective persons are assumed to be equally responsible except in the most extreme cases of coercion or mental distress. The notion that there might exist degrees of freedom and responsibility is not seriously entertained in law, and even where a doctrine of "diminished responsibility" has been instituted, the conditions which constitute diminished responsibility relate only to the most extreme end of the range of responsibility. Let us examine this "range of responsibility" more closely.

In his book entitled *Punishing Criminals*, Ernest van den Haag defends the traditional legal conception of responsibility, identifying variations it responsibility only at the extreme end of the range. In the example which follows he addresses the relationship between determinism, freedom, and responsibility by drawing a distinction between causation and compulsion His discussion is a classic example of the either/or mentality against which we are arguing. According to van den Haag:

> ...causation of one's behavior does not relieve it of its character as free choice or relieve the actor of responsibility for it unless the causation is compulsion ... To illustrate, I cause you to come to the forbidden place by asking you to—but you decide to let yourself be persuaded. Though it was caused (by my asking) you are responsible for your decision. My asking you is quite different from compelling by threatening to shoot you if you don't come; and the compelling threat is almost, but not quite, the same as forcing you by dragging you there without giving you any choice. Only in the last two cases are you not responsible— you were not free (van den Haag, 1975: 109).

This statement paints responsibility as a black and white (i.e., an either/or) issue. Either you are compelled and hence neither free nor responsible, or you are not compelled and hence both free and responsible. Then seems to be no middle ground. Let us stick with van den Haag's example to illustrate the drawbacks of viewing responsibility as an either/or proposition.

Suppose that instead of a single person asking one to come to the forbidden place, twenty persons were to make such a request. Absent physical force, one would still be "free" in the sense the "He/she decided to let his/herself be persuaded." But certainly twenty people asking represents more causation than if one person were to do so. However, there is still no compulsion. But what if 100 persons whom one trusts, and respects made such a request? And what about 200, or 1,000 such requests? On van den Haag's definition, there is still no compulsion. However, one sees that we approach the definition of compulsion, for the greater the peer pressure, the more coercive are the circumstances in which one must make one's decision. With twenty such requests, the refusal to enter the forbidden place does not come so easily, and with 100, it may not come at all!

Thus, the greater the peer pressure, the greater is the pressure to enter the forbidden place, or, the greater the peer pressure, the further we move along the continuum from causation to compulsion (though we may never actually reach the latter). To simply assert that anyone who doesn't have a gun at his head is not under compulsion and is therefore fully responsible in that he is "free" to decide to let himself be persuaded is to grossly oversimplify the complexities of interpersonal and situational inducements. Is it not strange that van den Haag acknowledges variance in the degree of compulsion (e. g. between the individual with the gun to his head and the person dragged without choice), but does not apply similar logic to degrees of causation?

The diagram that follows suggests that freedom and responsibility should be seen in continuous rather than in discrete terms. From this perspective it makes more sense to speak of degrees of freedom and responsibility, of people being more-or-less free rather than being free or not free. Turning once more to van den Haag's example, we would argue that the person subjected to 1,000 requests (person A) was under more deterministic pressure to enter the forbidden place than the person exposed to one such request (person B). Though both are still responsible because each retains the ability to choose, person A is less responsible than person B because she/he was exposed to a good deal more causation. Similarly, were Sartre's prisoner of war to confess under torture, he would be less responsible for his confession than the prisoner who willingly passed information to the enemy in order to receive special privileges.

RESPONSIBILITY CONTINUUM

No Responsibility			Responsibility
Compulsion	Coercion	Causation	Free Choice

Contrast this with the position we are arguing against, which suggests (a) that we are free if choice exists, and (b) that we are responsible if we could choose not to engage in the forbidden activity. Our position is that one has a choice if alternatives are present, but that freedom and responsibility are relative to both the number and type of alternatives available, and these in turn are structured relative to the "life choices" available to individual, by virtue of their position in the class structure. The difference is one between a discrete and a continuous definition of freedom and, consequently of responsibility. Let us summarize our position thus far.

1. Social class is largely responsible for defining the life chances available to persons at various locations in the social structure.
2. The number and type of life chances available to persons will directl3 influence the range and type of life choices they are able to make.

3. Because freedom and responsibility are relative to both the quantity and quality of available life choices, and because these choices van according to one's location in the class structure, they should be see' in continuous rather than either/or terms.

Taken together these three propositions constitute a sociology of structured choice. It is a "sociology" because it is concerned with the way everyday social interactions influence people to behave in certain ways, and it use the notion of "structure" to explain how the choices of specific individual in concrete circumstances are shaped by situational incentives, inducements and temptations. We believe it is a more sensible approach than one which flatly states that all people are equally free and equally responsible unless they can demonstrate compulsion or insanity.

The implication in all this is that social class has a great deal to do with structuring choices and, hence, with dispensing greater or lesser amounts of freedom and responsibility.

Choice, responsibility and criminality

Of two men who have committed the same theft, how much less guilty is he who scarcely had the necessaries of life than he who overflowed with excess? Of two perjurers, how much more criminal is he on whom one has striven from his childhood to impress feelings of honor, than he who, abandoned to nature, never received the benefit of education? (Marat in Foucault, 1978: 98).

Let us begin with von Hirsch's claim that impoverished defendants may be less culpable due to their deprived social status, and from the following rule of thumb offered by H. L. A. Hart (in von Hirsch, 1976: 145), which suggests that:

in general, a violator may be deemed less culpable if at the time of the offense he found himself, through no fault of his own, in a situation where conformity ... was a matter of special difficulty for him as compared with ... persons normally placed.

If we can successfully defend this thesis, then lower class persons should be considered less responsible for their crimes than more privileged persons committing the same offenses. Exactly how much less responsible, and what this means in policy terms, will be dealt with in the conclusion.

In presenting our argument we limit discussion to so-called instrumental crimes. Instrumental crimes are motivated by a rational or utilitarian concern to reap a material reward of some sort, and persons committing instrumental crimes calculate their potential gains in terms of cost-benefit considerations. Questions an "instrumental criminal" might ask before committing an offense include: What will I gain by such an offense? What might I lose? What are the chances of getting caught? These are cost-benefit type questions, and the rule of thumb is that persons will commit crimes if their social circumstances are such that they have more to gain and/or less to lose by doing so.

The next issue is: are there persons in our society for whom crime might be a rational choice (i.e., might be sensible in cost-benefit terms) given the number and type of life chances available to them? We believe the answer is yes, the reason being that there exist socially structured circumstances which provide certain groups with strong temptations and incentives to commit instrumental crimes. To make our point that (a) temptations to crime are situationally induced, and (b) that temptations and incentives are different for persons at different locations in the class structure, we shall use the economic concept of marginal utility and the cost-benefit logic of control theory.

The idea behind marginal utility suggests that the "marginal" value of a dollar decreases as the amount of money increases, and vice versa. For example, if one has only a dollar and receives an extra dollar, the marginal value of this additional dollar is fairly high, for the amount has doubled. On the other hand, if a millionaire were given a dollar, the marginal value of his extra dollar is next to nothing, for what is one dollar to a millionaire? From this economic concept one can derive a corollary proposition: that because they have less to begin with, a single dollar is worth more to poor persons than to wealthy ones. Let us examine the implications this has in terms of providing temptations and incentives for crime.

Because a single dollar is worth more to poor persons than to wealthy ones, there is a difference in the types of cost-benefit calculations made by these two groups. Since the dollar is worth more to those who have less, the prospect of an additional dollar will stimulate the "benefit" side of their cost-benefit calculation more than it will for wealthy persons whose additional dollar is not much of a benefit. In terms of crime, this scheme suggests that certain types of crime will be more attractive to persons who have fewer resources. More specifically, the increased marginal value of the dollar makes attractive to lower class persons those forms of criminality which yield the cash form of money (e. g., robbery, burglary, larceny), and these crimes are more easily discovered and more severely punished than are crimes of the powerful.

As other contributions to this volume make clear, privileged persons are also tempted to commit crimes, and the crimes they commit are more serious and more lucrative than lower class crimes (see also Reiman, 1984 Michalowski, 1985; Lynch and Groves, 1986; Frank, 1985). But there is an important difference here, for while the accumulation of money may be the bottom line for rich and poor alike, the form of money desired will certainly differ. The upper-class individual is less likely to commit crimes involving the cash form of money; these crimes are too visible, and the payoff is too small. This is why well-to-do offenders do not walk into gas stations with pistols. Given their social position, tax evasion, securities fraud, and price fixing are far more attractive; they do not involve cash transfers, and they yield far greater monetary rewards and far less in terms of punishment Thus, among the privileges which accrue to persons in advantaged locations in the class structure one must include the ability to commit crimes which command the greatest returns, yet at the same time are relatively immune from punishment.

The argument as presented thus far can be restated in the language of control theory as follows: When persons acquire more in terms of socially valued items such as prestige, power, and wealth, they are less likely to risk their privileges by engaging in common crimes such as burglary, robbery, or larceny. In simple cost-benefit terms, persona enjoying privileged life choices have more to lose and less to gain by committing street crimes which are more likely to be detected and, when detected, more likely to be punished.

Ernest van den Haag (1973) has addressed this differential temptation issue, and his position, at least in part, is very close to our own. Speaking to the idea that the incentives and temptations to commit crimes vary by social class, van den Haag (1973: 43-44) argues that:

> ...people differ, and so do the situations in which nature and society places them. So do, therefore, the degrees and kinds of opportunity, of temptation, of need, or stimulation to violate laws to which different people are exposed or by nature inclined...
> Often it is argued that justice would be more perfect if it were to pay more heed to the different living conditions, the different environments, of the rich and the poor, of the white

and the black, the educated and the uneducated... Such differences are real and immensely important, and they do lead to different temptations, of different intensity and to different opportunities for crime.

After noting the dynamics of determinism, social class, and the criminal alternative, van den Haag does not retreat on the question of criminal responsibility. He agrees that the unequal distribution of opportunities tempt some to commit crimes more than others but argues that this is irrelevant to the issue of responsibility. On van den Haag's logic, the only way socially structured deprivations could reduce responsibility is if they were "shown to produce seizures beyond the control of the poor which causes them to commit crimes ..." (van den Haag, 1973: 97).

The contrast with our own position could not be clearer. Having abandoned either/or logic, our own view is that persons who are more tempted are less responsible than those who are less tempted, or who are not tempted at all (note that we are not absolving anyone of responsibility, for even the strongly tempted bear some responsibility for their actions). van den Haag, on the other hand, argues that so long as persons can choose to refrain from engaging in criminal behavior, they are not to be relieved of any quantum of moral responsibility for their actions. As in the "forbidden place" example referenced earlier, van den Haag is able to acknowledge different degrees of determinism, but clings stubbornly to his two-value logic as regards responsibility.

In sum, the concept of marginal utility and the control theory emphasis on cost-benefit calculations helps explain why poor persons are more tempted to engage in instrumental criminal behaviors which (a) yield the cash form of money and (b) receive the most punishment. The key is to bear in mind that differential temptations are a function of the differentially distributed opportunities and incentives which largely determine the components of an individual's cost-benefit calculations. Viewed in this light, part of the responsibility for crime must be borne by socially structured situations themselves, for these situations expose certain persons to greater degrees of temptation than other groups whose location in the class structure is more favorable. As Newman (1985:198) argues in another context, privileged persons are "freer to choose not to engage in these [criminal] behaviors, and this freedom differential should not be discounted when trying to figure out "who deserves what" at punishment time.

Conclusion: attaining a semblance of justice

> People who have grown up in difficult surroundings...ought
> perhaps to be more leniently dealt with in respect to their trans-
> gressions than other people, ...not on the basis of any hope that it
> would help, but on the basis of a reasoned assessment that it
> would be a decent and just solution for one who has had such a
> difficult start in life. (Nils Christie, 1974: 294)

In philosophical terms the retributive formula for punishment
is quite clear: first, punish in proportion to the gravity of the
offense, and second, punish in proportion to the culpability of the
offender. However, in the "real world' figuring out how to distribute
punishment in a fair and just manner is not so easy, especially
when this real world is characterized by tremendous disparities
in life chances and choices. How do the unjust consequences of
social inequalities relate to retributive punishment?

The effects of inequality are, first, that even though their
crimes cost society more in economic and human terms, privileged persons do not receive the amount of punishment they
deserve; and second, that because their crimes are less serious,
and because they are less free not to commit these :rimes, persons
in deprived socio-economic circumstances deserve less punishment than their privileged counterparts, and, by implication, less
punishment than they currently receive. The question is: how can
we compensate for the effects of these inequalities at punishment
time?

Assuming a sentencing scheme where judges have some latitude
in considering aggravating and mitigating circumstances (i.e.,
indeterminate or presumptive sentencing), our specific proposal is
that extreme socioeconomic deprivation be considered a mitigating factor for persons found guilty of street crimes. Specifically, persons with an annual income of $6,000 or less, who
were unemployed at the time of their arrest, and who had less
than a high school education—all of which pretty well fit the
profile of persons now incarcerated in federal prisons—would be
eligible for automatic mitigation. Another possibility would be
that those who qualify as indigent (that is, two-thirds of all felony
defendants) would be so eligible (Inciardi, 1984).

Note that criminals are not being let off the hook here: assuming that the system has worked properly, we can also assume
that the vast majority of convicted persons are guilty—and
according to the logic of retributive theory, the guilty must be
punished. All we are asking is that (1) some mechanism be found

to compensate for unjust, class-based discrepancies in punishment, and (2) that in devising such a scheme we acknowledge that *part of the responsibility for crime lay with those social-structural circumstances which provide differential incentives and motivations for criminal behavior.*

In our estimation this is a modest and even a conservative proposal in two respects. First, the call for reform is conservative because it does not extend beyond the bounds of the criminal justice system, and second, mitigation is a modest adjustment in sentencing because it normally does not exceed 0% - 20% of the total sentence. Some will no doubt feel that this policy recommendation goes too far, others that it does not go far enough.. In defense of our proposal we argue that the proposed change would make for a fairer system than we have now. Absent prospects for meaningful reductions a social inequality in the foreseeable future, the proposal offered here offers something, and something is better than nothing (Platt, 1982).

7. On sentencing

Ernest van den Haag

The criminal law threatens persons who do what it prohibits with punishment in order to deter them from doing it. Would-be offenders see the threats of the criminal law as dangers. Most people, including most offenders, respond to dangers, be they natural or legal, by adapting their behavior so as to minimize risks. It would be hard to explain the survival of the human race otherwise.

The more severe or frequent punishment is, the greater the danger, the more it deters. However, no threat, no matter how great the danger it produces, can deter everybody. Some persons are altogether unresponsive to danger or even attracted by it. Many more are deterrable, but not deterred because current threats are insufficient. More severe threats, or threats more likely to be carried out, may deter them. Further, threats which deter persons only mildly attracted by criminal opportunities, or persons that have only minor criminal opportunities, will not suffice to deter those strongly attracted by crime, or all those who have major criminal opportunities. However, increases in the severity of threats and in the frequency with which they are carried out usually are limited by costs and by considerations of justice. if the innocent were threatened together with the guilty they would have no material reason to remain innocent. Hence the courts must discriminate, i.e., do justice. In doing so they cannot avoid acquitting offenders when the evidence is insufficient to demonstrate their guilt. Further, rules meant to restrain law enforcers from interfering with non-offenders also protect many offenders from search and apprehension. Hence, legal threats are not carried out often enough to deter offenders who might be deterred if threats of punishment were more frequently carried out.

Justice also requires us to attempt to proportion the size of each threatened punishment to the perceived gravity of the offense and to other threat so proportioned. Disproportionate punishments are felt to be unjust. However, the threat size required to successfully deter from an offense does not depend on its gravity, but on its attractiveness to prospective offenders. Whenever the attractiveness of the offense exceeds its perceived gravity threats, the sizes of which are proportioned to the gravity of the offense, an unlikely to deter those who might respond only to more severe threats, pro portioned to the crime's attractiveness. Further, the degree of attractiveness differs from person to person, so that threats can be tailored to it only in at imperfect fashion.

The "gravity" of crimes, to which punishment is to correspond roughly equals the intended and actual harm the crime does. But it is an uneasy compound of disparate ingredients, since the degree of wrongful intention or of any culpability, may be independent of the harm done and the two are not commensurable.

The perceived need for deterrence from an offense does not always coincide with its gravity. Adam Smith offers an example. A sentry is executed for falling asleep on his watch. The gravity of the offense is perceived as minor, but the need to deter from it as major. The need to deter prevail and this leads to a harshness Smith laments as necessary but unjust. However, when deterrence requires harshness and gravity does not, often gravity prevails as the criterion and we threaten but mild punishment. Our minor threats against drunken drivers who do harm—for that matter against an; drunks who do harm—may be just, considering the lack of malevolent intent but they do not satisfy the need for deterring drunken driving. Nor do our threats against juvenile offenders deter. Justice to offenders, proportioned to their culpability—which together with harmfulness determines gravity— often involves injustice to victims who might have been spared, if threat were harsher and thus more deterrent.

Since they bear no relation to social needs, punishments according to desert often are replaced by deterrent punishments. This occurs when the perceived need for deterrence is great and the punishment needed for deterrence is major while the deserved punishment is minor. Normally we will not severely punish a hungry person who steals food. However, if food is very scarce because of an emergency, we may threaten severe punishment because deterrence becomes important as the harm does. Still the culpability may not be greater than that of Adam Smith's sentry.

Societies do not always behave rationally in this respect to crime, although criminals do. Thus in the U. S., after a long decline in the crime rate, lasting into the 1950s, we experienced a great increase-232 percent between 1960-75. Burglary rates tripled. So did robbery rates. The homicide rate rose from 4.7 per 100,000 in 1961 to 10.2 per 100,000 in 1974. Half the increase in property crimes and 10 percent of the increase in violent crime is accounted for by the increased proportion of young males in the population. But, according to age specific crime rates, the remainder of the increase must be otherwise accounted for. The major factor was a decrease in the frequency and severity of punishment. The judiciary, instead of controlling crime by punishment, very nearly decontrolled it by non-punishment. Between 1960-70 the probability of being imprisoned for a felony decreased fivefold. The number of imprisoned persons fell from 112 per 100,000 to 70. Rehabilitative ideology may account for the judicial behavior at the time. Whatever the motive, the net rewards of crime were increased by reducing the risk of punishment, and crime rose consequently.

Although the threat of punishment deters, actual punishment is retributive, since it punishes only past offenses. Distribution of punishments deserved according to guilt is morally justified by concepts of retribution and desert. These concepts are essential to moral theories which help explain why the community prohibits, or should prohibit and punish, certain actions as wrong. However, rehabilitationists regard punishment according to guilt with misgivings. They would prefer a medical model, which makes guilt and justice irrelevant, substituting social and individual "needs for treatment" and dealing with crime as one deals with hepatitis. But they have not demonstrated that criminals are "sick," or that there is a cure called rehabilitation.

Further, if an act for which a reward was promised has been done, the promised reward must be given, regardless of how the person to whom the promise was made is likely to behave in the future. Future conduct is relevant only to future promises and rewards. Analogously, a threatened punishment must be imposed independently of the future conduct of the person against whom it was threatened. Future conduct is relevant only to future threats and punishments. Punishment, then, need not rest on anything but past threats; and it cannot rest on the desire for rehabilitation or incapacitation, i.e., on future conduct. Both may coincide with punishment; but they also may be separately produced; and punishment need not produce either.

Finally, although rehabilitation is incidental to punishment, punishment usually is essential to rehabilitation. Without punishment rehabilitation is unlikely to take place, for it is the experience of punishment, and the threat of future punishments, that may suggest to offenders that their criminal conduct is self-defeating; punishment gives them the main motive for rehabilitation. In the absence of such a motive, rehabilitation cannot be helped by any program of treatment. Punishment and the threat of punishment may not be sufficient, but they are necessary ingredients for rehabilitation. On the other hand, the rehabilitation of an offender is neither a necessary, nor a sufficient justification for stopping a punishment inflicted to carry out a threat against an offense he committed in the past.

*

However important in moral theory, desert, or retribution, need not play a role in the theory of punishment itself. The contrary belief rests on an insufficient distinction between moral and instrumental theories of punishment. Moral theories are theories of right and wrong, of desert, of good and bad. They morally justify ends and limit means, while instrumental theories concern the effectiveness of the latter.

Instrumental theories of punishment deal with social devices to control what moral theory tells us to control. Punishment and the threat of punishment are more or less effective means of social control, means used to accomplish the (moral) ends incorporated in the law. Thus in the theory of punishment moral concepts only play a limiting role. (Some means may be unacceptable though effective; they may cause more harm than justified by the ends they accomplish.) If one postulates that whatever the law prohibits be regarded as harmful or morally wrong, concepts such as desert are not needed in the instrumental theories of punishment which explain how law violations are affected by punishment. Deterrence suffices to explain both the size and distribution of threats and punishments.

Whatever their moral merit, retributionist theories, which explain and justify punishment as deserved or "just," are not needed to tell us (a) why we threaten, (b) why we punish, (c) why we punish only the guilty, and (d) why we threaten or punish them to the degree to which we do. According to Occam's razor— *essentia non sunt multiplicanda praeter neceesitatem* (concepts should not be multiplied beyond need)—retributionist theories are not needed within any causal (as distinguished from moral) discourse. The social need for deterrence alone can be shown to justify and to determine the size of penalties and their distribution exclusively to the guilty. A punishment is justified by deterrence, if threatening it suffices (and does not exceed) what is required to keep the rate of the threatened crime at the level desired by the community in view of the additional cost of additional reductions. In turn, the reasons for accepting a given crime rate, for not increasing threats, may be material or moral, as is the cost to be calculated.

The standard objection, that deterrence may be produced immorally, by punishing the innocent misrepresented as guilty attributes to deterrence theory a moral or immoral purpose which is not found in it. Deterrence theory merely describes the causal relation between threats, punishments and crime control. Unlike moral theories causal theories do not prescribe. Deterrence theory does not imply that crime control morally justifies particular punishments however effective, or the infliction of punishments on innocent persons misrepresented as guilty, however effective that may be. That infliction could be justified only by a moral principle that gives priority to deterrence over the legal evil of harming innocents intentionally, and over the moral evil of deception. Such a moral principle is not inherent in deterrence theory, or in any causal theory, although it may be consistent with moral theories such as utilitarianism, and inconsistent with others. Both are irrelevant to deterrence theory per se.

*

Confinement is not essential to punishment, since punishment may consist of a fine or, in the past, the infliction of pain. Nor is punishment essential to confinement, which may be imposed for non-punitive reasons on the insane, on those suffering from infectious diseases, or on those held for trial. Punishment is thus not a necessary reason for incapacitation, although a sufficient one.

Whereas punishment is threatened to deter, and imposed because threatened, incapacitation also may be imposed for reasons that have nothing to do with deterrence. If we knew, by revelation, that a man will throw a bomb to harm the community, we certainly would incapacitate him for as long as we knew him to be willing and capable of throwing the bomb, regardless of whether his intent is criminal or his mind is deranged. By incapacitating him we do not intend to punish him: he has done nothing, as yet, to justify punishment. We cannot punish anyone for what he has not yet done. We can incapacitate him, however, to prevent harm. Incapacitation, then, may be a measure of preemptive social defense, quite independent of punishment.

Now, in practice, certainty about what anyone will do is hard to come by. However, we have statistical probabilities which may vary from offender to offender and can be calculated. They indicate that those convicted of a second offense, particularly if young, are much more likely to commit other offenses than those who are not, and those convicted of a third offense are still more likely to continue criminal conduct. It is also statistically likely that those convicted of second and third offenses have committed other offenses of which they were not convicted.

The punishment threatened for committing a second offense should exceed that threatened for the first. The community may wish to deter offenders not only from specific offenses, but also from continued offending. The community may rely on offenses committed, combined with other relevant factors, to statistically predict the likelihood of further offenses. Where such likelihood is found to be considerable and to significantly exceed the average likelihood of future offenses by non-convicts, the convict likely to commit further offenses of sufficient harmfulness might well be incapacitated for as long as that likelihood remains high. (This may justify the incapacitation of some young recidivists up to the age of forty. Some older recidivists may be incapacitated up to the age of fifty, if our data relating age and likelihood of criminality are correct (Nettler, 1974: 99-101).

There are two major arguments against imposing added incapacitation on convicted offenders on the basis of categorical (statistical) prediction of recidivism.

By imposing such incapacitation we punish for what will or might be done, not for what has been done. This argument either fails to distinguish between incapacitation and punishment, despite the conceptual difference noted, or, more often, relies on the fact that the incapacitated person understandably will feel punished because he is deprived of liberty by the decision of a social authority. Yet, although the purpose may be preventive the added incapacitation is part of what was threatened part, if you will, of the punishment threatened. The offender is incapacitated for continuing in his criminal conduct. Unlike the insane, he was able to avoid the threatened incapacitation by avoiding the second offense.

Note here that a punishment can be harsh or mild, useful or useless. But, if threatened, it cannot be unjust. By committing the crime, the offender knowingly volunteered for the risk of suffering the threatened punishment. Thus, the punishment is no more "unjust" than an injury suffered in a fall by a man who volunteered to climb a mountain. Both the mountain climber and the criminal volunteered for the risk of the punishment that befell them.

In war we shoot at enemy soldiers who individually may not be guilty of anything, not even of being hostile to our country or cause. Yet we can defend our country and prevent harm to it only by shooting enemy soldiers who otherwise might shoot us. Social defense against internal enemies admittedly is different from social defense against external enemies. For one thing, less is at stake for the country as a whole. But there are similarities as well. In either case we must defend the community against harm by incapacitating and deterring both actual and potential enemies. Those who have enlisted in the criminal army are personally more guilty than those who serve in the enemy army. Criminals are volunteers; they usually serve no cause but their own advancement, whereas enemy soldiers usually are draftees, who do not serve to advance their personal fortunes. But both criminals and enemy soldiers must be incapacitated as long as we have reason to believe that they will harm us if free to do so. Prolonged incapacitation is among the risks second offenders volunteer for. It is less of a risk and more easily avoidable than the risk the draftee runs.

In sentencing previous arrests as well as prior convictions may be regarded as aggravating factors. Arrests which did not lead to convictions do not, of course, demonstrate guilt. But they should have warned the defendant that he is suspected of criminal conduct. If, despite such warning, he does commit the offense of which he is now convicted, it suggests a stronger commitment to criminality than if he had not been arrested and let go before his conviction. That conviction, in a sense, justifies the fruitless arrests which the offender failed to heed as a warning. He should be held responsible for that stronger commitment.

An argument against prolonged incapacitation to reduce recidivism, more cogent than arguments based on justice, rests on our limited ability to predict. If not incapacitated, perhaps a majority of recidivists, statistically likely to commit additional offenses, may never actually do so; at least they may never be convicted of other crimes. Statistical predictions can be improved, but it is unlikely that they will ever approach certainty. Further added incapacitation per se is not necessarily all that useful. It is useful in as much as it deters, because it is felt to be additional punishment. But with incapacitation, it probably has limited usefulness. Although in practice fused with deterrence, incapacitation can theoretically be distinguished from it. If we make the distinction, we may realize that the crime rate depends exclusively on the expected net gains from crime, compared to the net gain from legitimate activities available to offenders. This ratio is not changed by incapacitation *per se*. Thus, if all practicing prostitutes in New York were incapacitated, the rate of prostitution in New York would, within a short time, return to what it was before, as long as the net gain from prostitution is not reduced. There are always more persons capable of committing crime than do. Any deactivation of practicing car thieves will increase the price, of stolen cars and attract new ones into the trade, as the deactivation of practicing prostitutes would. Even the frequency of non-market-dependent crimes, such as rape, depends on the net gain. It is largely determined by the, cost of crime to the criminal imposed by the courts. All this argues against attributing the crime reducing effect of added punishment to incapacitation it is due to deterrence. The mistaken attribution can make a difference. But that difference need not detain us here.

*

Juveniles who have committed acts defined as crimes when committee by adults, should be tried and sentenced by the same courts adults are tried by, and under the same laws. If counsel for the defense wishes to plead diminished capacity for *mens rea*, or any other legal excuse or mitigating circumstance, he can do so. But the law and the court should not assume priori that the age of juveniles is a mitigating circumstance, let alone a legs excuse. There is no evidence to indicate that all juveniles, owing to their age, are unaware of the gravity of their offenses or unlikely to be deterred by threats. However, juveniles cannot be deterred (or, for that matter, rehabilitated) by promising them immunity from serious punishment, as we have done hitherto. And they are not less, and often more, socially dangerous than older offenders.

*

There never was a justification for having sentences second-guessed by parole boards. They know nothing the sentencing judge could not know, except for information about the offender's conduct in prison. Such conduct is not relevant to the punishment to which he has been sentenced because of his offense; and conduct in prison does not predict future conduct outside prison. Hence parole should be abolished. It rests on considerations that, apart from being materially wrong, are irrelevant under the justice and the deterrence criterion. All sentences should be for a determinate period, fixed by the court, and flat, i.e., not modifiable to parole boards, whose remaining task would be the post-release supervision of convicts. Some credit for good conduct in prison, given at the discretion of prison authorities, may help prison discipline, but should not significantly modify sentences. The maximum credit given should not exceed ten percent of the sentence—otherwise indeterminacy would be reintroduced.

To be deterrent, sentences must be predictable, and the relevant prediction refers to the time that actually must be served. Therefore, all punishment should be mandatory, reducing judicial discretion as much as possible. Judges should be able to reduce or increase the mandatory sentences by no more than ten percent. If a judge wishes to go beyond this, because of circumstances he deems exceptional, he may do so, but his sentence should be automatically reviewed by an appeals court, empowered to let it stand, or to re-impose the mandatory sentence. When neither seems satisfactory, the appeals court may ask the lower court to reconsider the sentence. However unless the discretionary limits are exceeded, sentences should not be appeal. able. Giving judges the discretion they currently have, does not adapt the sentence to the personality of the criminal, as was hoped, but to that of the judge. Both adaptations lead to disparate sentences perceived as arbitrary and capricious. Both reduce the deterrent effect of punishment which depends on predictability. Hence, discretion should be narrowly limited.

Probation and suspended sentences should be available only to first offenders, for comparatively minor offenses. If judges grant probation in other circumstances, the sentence should be automatically reviewed by a higher court empowered to reject it.

*

It may be argued that the sentencing criteria suggested would increase intolerably the shortage of prison space. Undoubtedly the increasing severity of sentences, which is already occurring, requires more prison space than is presently available. Enactment of the reforms proposed here temporarily may require still more. How much additional prison space will be required permanently is hard to predict. If more severe and frequent prison sentence: are given, a higher proportion of offenders will be in prison. But if these sentences deter, fewer offenses will be committed. Thus, the total number of offenders may decrease and the actual prison population ultimately may too.

Yet, at least temporarily, more prisons will have to be built. It has beer argued that this will be too costly. However, it is cheaper to build prisons than to tolerate a higher crime rate, even though taxpayers, rather than crime victims, may have to bear the cost of building. At any rate, the cost of imprisonment is far higher than it need be for three reasons, apart from waste and corruption.

(1) Attempts are made to provide prisoners with rehabilitative service: and amenities which have never been shown to contribute to any of the purposes of punishment, including rehabilitation. Television is not required as part of humane treatment, or of rehabilitation; nor is tennis, or conjugal sex. A prisoner is intentionally severed from amenities. There is no reason then, to provide them at government expense. Further, if his normal environment were helpful in producing lawful behavior, he probably would not be in prison. Hence building prisons on costly real estate, near urban centers to facilitate visits from relatives and friends, is unnecessary. If the amenities unrelated to the penal purpose of prisons were not provided imprisonment could be less costly without becoming inhumane.

Prisoners are not given productive work. They are thus not allowed to earn enough to pay for their keep. Most legal experts are in favor, as I am, of normal wages and work opportunities for prisoners, and of incentive pay. Even non-monetary work incentives, such as shortening of sentences according to work performed are not altogether inconsistent with deterrent punishment, if kept within narrow limits. I will not dwell on this matter. Obstacles come from labor unions and business; the problem is political. But it must be noted that prisons are costly only because we insist on making them costly. They could be self-supporting and, if prisoners became taxpayers, they could increase government revenue. Lawful work at normal wages within prisons may even be rehabilitative. It is one "treatment" that has never been seriously tried.

The most costly part of imprisonment consists of the measures taken to prevent escapes. These measures also raise prison building costs. However, not all inmates are violent, or prone to escape. They may have surrendered voluntarily and may prefer to serve their time rather than to add to their crimes by escaping and living as fugitives. Accordingly, we should create some small prisons with minimal supervision and not much more security than is provided in a factory. Roll calls will be needed—but no actual measures to prevent flight. In doubtful cases prisoners working in these prisons may provide bonds, forfeited if they try to escape. If only the actual security risks—violent or escape-prone prisoners (a category which may include all young offenders sentenced to long terms)—are kept in high security prisons, imprisonment will become cheaper than it is now.

Those who most lament prison crowding and wax eloquently about the inhumane conditions it creates are often the very persons who did their best, for ideological reasons, to prevent the building of additional prisons. They have helped create the conditions which they now use to insist that offenders should not be confined as often, or as long, as is needed to deter from crime. Most of them persist in opposing the building of prisons. I have found it impossible to rehabilitate them.

8. Power concentration, legitimation crisis and penal severity

Martin Killias*

In the past ten years, criminal justice research on sanctions has dwelt on alternatives to imprisonment[1] and theories on the stable level of punishment in a given society (e.g., Blumstein and Cohen, 1973). Despite available alternatives, and "homeostasis" theories to the contrary, the incarceration rates of many countries continue to increase; the American rate of sentenced prisoners in State and Federal institutions rose between 1972 and 1979 by about 45 percent (Hindelang et al., 1981: Table 6.16), reaching its highest level in history (Cahalan, 1979). These rates should provoke more interest in research on variations in the levels of punishment, and concomitantly, in theories that explain variations in, rather than the stability of, punishment. Such theories could be used to address the question of the notoriously enormous cross-national differences in incarceration rates—a phenomenon largely ignored in stability of punishment theories, although some cross- sectional research has been conducted on fluctuations of incarceration rates (e. g., Blumstein, Cohen and Nagin, 1977; Blumstein and Moitra, 1979).

Theoretical framework

Theories that explain variations in the level of punishment fall into two basic, if simplistic, classifications: those that emphasize social structural variables, such as modernization and power concentration, and those that point to the amount of social conflict, measured by indicators of social crisis such as unem-

---

[1] Checking the subject indexes of the *Criminology and Penology Abstracts* (1978-1980):18-20, the author found more than 120 references concerning publications on alternatives to imprisonment, but only about 15 references concerning the incarceration rates and the continued use of imprisonment.

ployment. The following sections summarize the basic statements of both perspectives, and then attempt to integrate the two
by using the more abstract concept of legitimation.

The social structural perspective

In an article entitled "Two Laws of Penal Evolution,"[2] Durkheim
presented three hypotheses on variations in penal severity that are
far more specific than his much better known statements in *The
Division of Labor in Society* and *The Rules of Sociological Method.*[3]

First, Durkheim assumed that penal severity decreases with
development, since crime in primitive societies offended deeply
felt religious commands rather than individual, secular interests.
Second, he hypothesized that imprisonment would become the
dominant form of punishment in modern societies because they,
in contrast to primitive societies, would *have* the resources at
hand to construct and operate penitentiaries. Third, he stated that
penal severity reaches a peak every time the form of government
becomes "absolute," i.e. whenever power is highly concentrated
within a society. In line with his predilection for considering
religion as an independent variable, Durkheim explains this
relationship by the tendency of such governments to usurp a
religious authority, an example being kings who claimed to be
God's governors on earth, the "divine right of kings." Whether
religion per se is really the key variable in explaining penal severity,
or whether the key is that religious authority was usurped by
absolutist governments to legitimize extreme degrees of power
concentration, does not concern us, since power concentration in
itself might be a sufficient cause of an increase in penal severity.
This was also the position of Montesquieu, who had advanced
an almost identical hypothesis 150 years before Durkheim (Montesquieu, 1748/1977: book VI, ch. 6 and 13).[4]

---

[2] This article appeared first in *Annee Sociologique* 4 (1900): 65-95.

[3] This lack of attention to Durkheim's most specific writing on penal
severity may be due to the fact that it was not translated into English
until 1969, whereas his main works have been accessible in English
for at least a generation longer.

[4] Although it seems unlikely that Durkheim did not know this reference, he
does not quote Montesquieu's statement on the impact of "tyrannical"
forms of government on penal severity.

The conflict perspective

As one of the first writers on penal severity, Sorokin (1937/ 1962: 599-606) explained its variations by the amount of conflict within a given society. To illustrate his point, Sorokin presented data from France and Russia that revealed very high numbers of executions in times of serious civil disorder and revolution. Sorokin ascribed these fluctuations to a lack of consensus on basic cultural values, i.e. to attempts by the powerful to enforce their cultural standards against "oppositional" (sub-)cultural groups (1962: 598599). Being an adherent of the culture conflict approach, Sorokin did not differentiate between culture and social structure, or power and values.[5] Although his evidence does indicate that penal severity increased in times of social crisis, it seems that in these instances the power structure, rather than society's basic values, was in trouble. Besides, it does not seem feasible that fundamental differences with respect to crimes such as robbery, theft, murder, and rape could have reached such dramatic dimensions within such a short time, disappearing once the crisis had passed, as Sorokin's time-series suggests.[6] Therefore, theories that explain social crises in terms of strain within the social structure may account better for such peaks of penal severity.

Following the Marxian tradition of restricting the analysis to economic variables, Rusche and Kirchheimer (1939) claimed that the forms of punishment used by elites to control the lower classes are determined by criteria of economic rationality. Capital and corporal punishments are, therefore, presumed to prevail in societies suffering from a large surplus of manpower whereas imprisonment and forced labor are said to be the dominant forms of punishment whenever the scarcity of manpower makes them most profitable to the rulers. Accordingly, Rusche and Kirchheimer explained the decline of imprisonment during the second half of the 19th century by the decreasing profitability of forced labor.

---

[5] On this general deficiency of culture conflict theory, see Kornhauser (1978: 10-12).

[6] This assumption of dissent even regarding such basic crime concepts is a typical feature of culture conflict theory and is not supported by empirical evidence. See on this the literature review of Kornhauser (1978: 216-226). Interestingly, Sorokin himself expresses doubts regarding the feasibility of this assumption, and he criticizes some sociologists for having overstated the relativity of serious crimes (Sorokin, 1937/1982: 577).

They had some difficulty, however, in explaining the continued wide-spread use of imprisonment after World War I, i.e. during a time of high unemployment when capital punishment would have been, according to their theory, more in order to maximize profit by minimizing costs. Using an interpretation Rusche had advanced in an earlier paper (Rusche, 1933), they assumed that the increased power and organization of lower class persons had made a wide-spread return to capital punishment impossible. Modern authors, such as Quinney (1977) and Melossi and Pavarini (1979), emphasize again the role of the labor market and view imprisonment as a mechanism for reducing unemployment. Seeing the factory and the prison as complementary institutions to control the lower class,[7] they seem to base their reasoning on an implicit incapacitation model.

On empirical grounds, evidence concerning the labor market hypothesis has been mixed. On one hand, a number of studies identify an impressive impact of the unemployment rate on the use of imprisonment in capitalist societies (e.g., Jankovic, 1977; Greenberg, 1977; Yeager, 1979), although this relationship did not hold during the Great Depression (Jankovic, 1977) or in a cross-sectional study of American states (Garofalo, 1979).[8] However evidence does not support the concomitant assumption that imprisonment rates have an effect on levels of unemployment (Jankovic, 1977). This is not very surprising when one considers the proportions of these two variables. Whenever unemployment reaches a substantial level, say five or ten percent of the work force, the incarceration rate cannot affect it even in the slightest

---

[7] Melossi and Pavarini (1979: 246) express the alternative character of prison and factory in these words: "La fabbrica a per l'operaio come un carcere ...il carcere per l'internato e come una fabbrica." ("For the worker, the factory is like a prison, and for the prisoner, the prison is like a factory.")

[8] The American unemployment rate is calculated on the basis of those who report having actively looked for work during the recent past, and thus excludes from the work force those who have given up looking for a job. It may be a more valid indicator of fluctuation. over time than of cross-sectional differences, because the number of people who have given up looking for work may be particularly high in areas and among groups with chronically high unemployment. The differential validity of the measure of unemployment may account for the paradox that the latter is strongly correlated with imprisonment rates in time-series analyses, but not in Garofalo's cross-sectional study.

way, since nowhere does it exceed one half of a percent of the total population. This may also account for the negative correlation between unemployment and incarceration which Jankovic (1977) found during the Great Depression, when the immense increase in unemployment could not be followed any longer by a parallel increase in admissions to overcrowded prisons. Besides this more or less contemporary evidence, the available historical data on execution rates[9] do not leave any room for the assumption that the death penalty has never been used to control the labor market (Steinert and Treiber, 1978). It seems that the elites maintained social order by the threat of capital punishment rather than by large-scale executions (Hay, 1975), which might or might not have been economically rational.

In modern industrialized societies government is expected to promote the citizens' welfare, and this usually includes the notion of full employment. One may assume, therefore, that high unemployment rates adversely affect the legitimation of those in power. Incarcerating more people for longer periods of time, i.e. "getting tough on criminals," can be a response to the crisis effect of unemployment, rather than an attempt, in and of itself, to ease labor market oversupply. If this holds true, one can expect incarceration rates to rise whenever the social order undergoes a period of crisis, whether this crisis is due to high unemployment rates or to factors located in the political sphere, i.e. within the "superstructure" of a given system. Greenberg (1980) illustrates the relevance of such factors in a study of Poland's highly fluctuating imprisonment rates. Although he could not find any

---

[9] Figures given in this context are usually exponentially overstated, or are based on extremely unreliable sources. The often cited figure of 72-80,000 thieves executed under Henry VIII (see, e.g., R.usche and Kirchheimer, 1939) were simply a fantastic invention of a very dubious individual (for details see Aydelotte, 1913: 5). The same is true of the 20-30,000 death sentences which Benedictus Carpzovius, a famous 17th century judge and criminal law professor in Leipzig, was often said to have pronounced. Boehn (1940-42) revealed that the real figure was at least 100 times lower, and Leipzig had a particularly low execution rate during Carpzovious' office, namely about .35 per 10,000 population during the period of 1652-1688. The figures given by Steinert and Treiber (1978), and calculations by the author, reveal that the execution rates did not exceed 2 per 10,000 in any of the cities considered, even during periods of the most extensive use of capital punishment (i.e., at the end of the 16th century).

correlation with the situation in the labor market, the changes in the incarceration rate seemed to be closely related to political events, especially the political crises Poland underwent in 1956 and again in 1968.

Studying incarceration rates as depending on crises within the political and social sphere would overcome the "economic reductionism" (Greenberg, 1980) of many Marxist criminologists. And considering unemployment as a crisis factor, too, makes it possible to integrate the labor market approach with Sorokin's version of the conflict hypothesis, if the latter is seen as a political crisis hypothesis, thereby dropping its underlying culture conflict assumptions. Of course, the concept of crisis needs more clarification, and this will be attempted in the following section.

Legitimation crisis and penal severity

Any power has a certain need for self-justification, as Max Weber stated some fifty years ago (Weber, 1925/1954: 335). This self-justification car be accomplished by investments the ruler makes to induce his subjects to believe that the power gap between he and them is ultimately in their best interests. He can, for example, settle social issues that previously seemed unsolvable, thereby leaving the impression of having quasi-magical capacities, or, as Weber would say, of having charismatic authority. Or he can base his position on a very long-lasting tradition, thereby giving his power the appearance of eternity and unavoidability, which in turn may deny the feasibility of any alternative. Finally, he can emphasize the expertise of him and his staff, thereby evoking the impression that his rule is based on profound wisdom which will lead to the best possible results for everybody, a least in the long run.

Such justifications of power can not only be identified at the macro sociological level, but can also be observed in social psychological studies of power legitimation in smaller groups (Wallster et al., 1973). For example power positions in the work place tend to be legitimized by referring to some sort of an investment status, such as education, seniority, expertise, overtime etc. Reasoning at the societal level, Heintz (1972: 140) hypothesizes that the legitimation of power becomes more difficult the more the power gap between the ruler(s) and the subordinates grows. In other words, the chance that a legitimation crisis will increase proportionately with power concentration. Besides, a legitimation crisis is likely to develop whenever the assumptions which justify the power structure are largely under-mined. This de-legitimation may occur because an alternative to the present power structure gains in popularity; however, the foremost cause may be the ruler' failure to meet the expectations which emanate from the assumptions that justify his power position. For example, the continued failure to provide full emp-loyment may in the long run seriously affect the legitimation of a social order previously assumed by those within it to be best suited to promote their welfare.

Legitimizing assumptions may certainly be important sources of power, since they motivate subordinates to comply without the ruler having to turn to force. This is not to argue that legitimation and force are opposite extremes of the same dimension, or that force will automatically be employed to defend a given power structure whenever its legitimation becomes problematic (Luh-mann, 1975: 68-69).[10] If power is conceived as a phenomenon of interaction rather than as a consequence of material resources (Luhmann, 1975: 9; Schneider, 1978: 35), it becomes obvious that power is more often created and maintained by the threat of force rather than by its actual use (Luhmann, 1975: 60-69). The steps through which a legitimation crisis is transformed into an increase in penal severity (not only in legal codes, but also in practice) needs, however, more clarification.

If de-legitimation of the existing power structure leads to an open challenge of the ruler(s), it seems plausible that the actual use of force, including that which is institutionalized in the criminal justice system, will increase. Thus, the violent response of the ruler to the violence of his opponents is reflected in peaks of executions, such as those in Prance and Russia reported by Sorokin (1937/1962: 601-603), and in high numbers of political prisoners. But why should any regime answer to a general legitimation crisis by emphasizing some form of "war on crime" which, *as* Wilkins (1976) noted, notoriously boils down to a "war on criminals?" Does non-political street crime threaten any government? As Taylor (1980) noted in an analysis of electoral campaigns in Britain and Canada, the conservative parties' law and order stances may be understood as an attempt to reduce the legitimation crisis of the given social order, since focusing on street crime has at the same time the effect of directing the

---

[10] Luhmann's work on power is also available in English: Niklas Luhmann, *Trust and Power,* (New York: Wiley, 1979).

public's attention away from potentially delegitimizing issues, such as unsettled economic problems, and of creating a climate of discipline and work-ethic, thus rallying the law-abiding majority in defense of the given order against "criminals" and all kinds of deviants. This emphasis on discipline, work, family, and moral order, a general feature of dictatorships of any political orientation, can be found even during times of revolutionary unrest when one would expect political opponents to be the only targets of a general crackdown. As the frequent executions of homosexuals, prostitutes, and other deviants in Iran illustrate, a substantial number of the victims of such waves of repression seem to be "immoral" rather than politically dangerous. It therefore seems that, given wide agreement on the undesirability of (street) crime, law and order politics are a way to increase consensus within a society, just as going to war against neighbors may be an efficient way to reduce interior dissent. But "war on crime" (or criminals) is of course, much less risky, and thus more attractive. Whenever politicians make crime an electoral or political issue, they may be doing so in a search for legitimation rather than because they really fear criminals. The increase in penal severity emanating from law and order policies may thus be the side effect of a search for consensus rather than an end in itself.

How can we predict that a legitimation crisis will arise, to be followed by an increase in penal severity? We may expect that the probability of *a* legitimation crisis and, concomitantly, of a rise in penal severity, will occur when:

- rulers cannot meet the standards which emanate from their own self-justification, and/or
- the power gap between rulers and their subordinates grows, i.e. when power is concentrated among a few.[11]

These two hypotheses are derived from the proposition that legitimation crises lead to increases in penal severity. And since the first hypothesis integrates earlier research from the conflict perspective, whereas the *second* restates Durkheim's and Montesquieu's power concentration hypothesis, one may conclude that the concept of legitimation crisis makes possible the integration

---

[11] This second hypothesis is supported by social psychological studies that found positive correlations between the power distance and punitive attitudes among the powerful toward their subordinates (Mulder, 1960; Kipnis, 1972).

of these two seemingly contradictory perspectives. However, Durkheim's main hypothesis, namely that penal severity decreases with modernization, will be discussed separately, as the concept of legitimation does not embrace modernization.

Research design

Cross-national analysis

Most research on penal severity has been based on historical and time-series analyses of criminal justice policies within one or, in some cases, a very few societies.[12] Such research designs have the advantage of allowing consideration of a large number of independent variables, and are less troubled with the problematic nature or, even worse, the unknown validity of the indicators used. On the other hand, being directed toward interpreting and explaining rather than predicting development, such studies tend to be less conclusive, and inferences regarding other societies remain rather speculative. Of course, it is not very meaningful to argue for or against the superiority of either of these two approaches since both serve an important function in the development of social science. Given the preponderance of time-series and historical studies on penal severity, the present study has been designed to analyze this topic using a sample of as many nations as possible.

The dependent variable

Penal severity can be operationalized in two different ways. First, we can look at the forms of punishments the judiciary has at its disposal, and compare different nations by using an underlying scale of penal severity. Second, we can consider the severity within a given form of punishment, e. g. by looking at the length of imprisonment or the amounts of fines. Both of these operationalizations have to cope with Christie's (1968) version of the stability of punishment hypothesis. According to Christie, the change in punishments over the past 200 years cannot be attributed to humanitarianism, nor to a decrease in society's punitiveness, but to a shift in the underlying scale of penal values. In other words, what once may have been "worth" the death penalty

---

[12] Sorokin's study, e.g., was based on a comparative and historical analysis of five societies (Russia, Germany, Austria, France, Italy). More recently, Ted R. Gurr et al., *Th Politics of Crime and Conflict: A Comparative History of Four Cities*, (Beverly Hills, Calif.: Sage Publications, 1977) used a very similar research design.

may, according to modern standards, only deserve five years in prison, and what once may have deserved imprisonment, may today be equivalent to a fine. Christie explains this shift in penal values by an increase in susceptibility, so that our (supposedly more lenient) punishments cause the same amount of suffering as did the more cruel ones of the past. Although such a shift in susceptibility and penal values may indeed have occurred, it seems unwarranted to infer from this that societies do not differ in penal severity, but only in penal values, since there seems to exist an immanent rank ordering of different forms of punishment which is valid across historical periods and national boundaries.

The relative severity of different forms of punishment can be assessed in a generally valid way by using their position within the process of pardoning, i.e., by looking at which form of punishment is commuted to what. In all the societies and in all the periods on which we are sufficiently informed, there is a consistent pattern: qualified forms of capital punishment are commuted into "simple" forms of the death penalty, imprisonment is used as a substitute for executing the offender, long imprisonment terms are reduced t(shorter ones, and prison sentences tend to be commuted to non-incarcerative sanctions, such as fines.[13] It seems, therefore, warranted to say that societies whose laws provide for the death penalty are characterized by more penal severity than abolitionist ones, and that societies using longer prison term; for the same kind of offenses are more punitive than others.

Regarding the use of imprisonment, penal severity is, in the absence of more adequate data, usually measured by comparing incarceration rates This way of operationalizing penal severity has to cope, however, with the objection that these data reflect nothing more than different levels of crime Although it would be an overstatement to say that crime rates do not hay(any impact on incarceration rates, the available evidence, nevertheless, sup ports Wilkins' (1965: 85) assumption that this impact is not too

---

[13] Of course, the relative severity of different sanctions may overlap at the lower and the upper ends, respectively, as in the case of very short imprisonment and very high fine! It may be difficult to rank some minor sanctions, such as withdrawal of a driver's license or, to cite an historical example, the temporary exclusion from the sacraments whirl according to Carpzovius (1652: pare II, quaestio 69, n. 55), was considered in Saxonia more severe punishment than a short prison sentence.

large. For. example, there is some indication that Eastern European countries haw lower crime rates than Western Europe (Kaiser, 1976; Shelley, 1981), but at the same time they have some of the highest incarceration rates in the world. In a number of studies (e.g. Doleschal 1979) the median time serve(by prisoners in different countries was compared with the incarceration rate of these nations, and there seems to be a strong trend for countries with high incarceration rates to punish their criminals with much longer prison terms.[14] Besides, studies on the incarceration rate in America consistently find a weak or, at best, a moderate correlation between incarceration and crime rates.[15]

The best way to assess the validity of incarceration rates as measures of penal severity would be to use crime rates as a control variable. For most of the countries that figure in our

---

[14] The median time served in American State prisons was 17.3 months in 1977 *(Characteristics of the Parole Population, 1978,* San Francisco: NCCD, 1980). In some state however, this time is considerably longer, as in California, where the median time *serve was* 34 months in 1976 for men, and 25 months for women, respectively (Brewer et al 1981). In contrast, the corresponding figure for the Netherlands is about 1 month, for Sweden 3 months (Doleschal, 1979), and for Switzerland about 3 months (Strafurfeile *der Schweiz, 1979,* Convictions in Switzerland, ed. Swiss Federal Statistical Office, Bern 1981). In interpreting these figures, one should keep in mind that the American figure do not include the far shorter sentences served in jails; on the other hand, Europea countries seem to restrict the use of imprisonment considerably more than the America states (Clinard, 1978: 116-117; Gillespie, 1980). It is not possible to determine to wh: degree these differences in the meaning of figures on time served in prisons affect the comparability, but it would seem that the exclusion of jails from the American data and the more conservative use of imprisonment in European countries tend to compensate for each other.

[15] Using time-series, Biles (1979) and Bowker (1981) found contradictory results concerning the relationship between crime rates and rates of imprisonment in State and Federal prisons. Using ordinal data, Nagel (1977) found a correlation of only .214 between rates of incarceration in State and Federal prisons and crime rates across the 50 states. Garofalo (1979), using a more comprehensive measure of incarceration which included jails and juvenile institutions, found correlations of .24 for property crime and .61 for violent crime rates. Using a similar measure of incarceration, the author found that total crime rates in 1971 and 1977 accounted for only 10 percent of the total variation in incarceration rates in 1972 and 1978, respectively, across the 50 states.

sample, the United Nations has gathered data on the number of offenses reported to the police and of identified offenders during the years 1970-1975. Unfortunately, these data are not published and could not be obtained for the present analysis.[16] In an unpublished analysis of these data, however, Newman and Vetere (1978) found a correlation between the rate of adult offenders recorded by the police and the incarceration rate of only .08, a finding that is all the more remarkable since offender as well as prisoner rates are based on persons.[17] Interpreting this finding, Newman and Vetere suggest that some countries may process and record a high number of offenders, yet punish them with non-incarcerative sanctions or short prison sentences, thereby keeping the incarceration rate at a relatively low level. Other countries, in contrast, may process far fewer people, but punish them very harshly which, in turn, increases the incarceration rates. In sum, this finding strongly supports Wilkins' (1974) statement that incarceration rates reflect penal severity rather than crime rates.[18]

The independent variables

The legitimation crisis in the form of a failure of the government to meet expectations emanating from its own self-justification has, in the present study, been operationalized by the unemployment rate. As mentioned above this indicator has been used by many other writers on incarceration and penal severity, although as a part of a different theoretical framework.

As indicators of power concentration, whose relevance in the present con text has been explained above, two different measures were used. First, the degree of power concentration at the govern-mental level has been assesses by distinguishing between countries

---

[16] 'The report published by the United Nations on this survey *(Crime Prevention and Control,* Report of the Secretary-General, 32nd session of the General Assembly, A/32/199, 22 September 1977) contains only aggregated data. For any meaningful analysis, crime and offender data should, however, be available at the level of countries rather than continents.

[17] Similarly, Greenberg (1977) found in a time-series analysis on Canada no correlation between conviction rate and prison admission rate.

[18] Since the rate of offenders, as a control variable would have to be introduced into the regression equation before the other independent variables, the fact that it accounts for less than 1 percent of variation in prisoner rates means that the omission of these data does not affect the results seriously.

having democratic and those with non-democratic forms of government. The criterion for this classification has been whether the executive and/or the parliament have been elected in free, open vote, i.e. according to the one-man-one-vote principle, in which the candidates number more than the available seats. Consequently, military governments, one-party regimes, and absolute monarchies have been classified as non-democratic. One may criticize this indicator on the grounds that it is rather crude; on the other hand, it seems closer to the concept of power concentration than indexes which also include several civil liberties,[19] and it seems to imply to a lesser degree a moral distinction between "good" any "bad" governments. Second, power concentration within a society has also been measured by Corrado: Gini's index of income concentration. This index can assume values between 0, indicating a perfectly equal income distribution, and 1.0, indicating concentration of all income at the top.[20] In Western societies, the Gini index is generally considered a very valid measure of power concentration, given the high correlation between wealth and power in capitalist countries. In communist nations, however, power may be associated with bureaucratic (dispositional) competences rather than with possession (Djilas, 1957: 44-46), and even chances to acquire consumer goods may be' less a function of income than in capitalistic countries (Weede, 1981). With income distribution not being a valid measure of power concentration under the communist system, and in line with recent research in this field (Weede 1981), no data on income distribution from communist countries have been analyzed in the present study.

Since both the form of government and the income concentration are highly correlated with social development (Bollen, 1979; Bornschier, 1978: the annual per capita national income has been introduced as a control variable. This measure is generally considered a more valid single indicator of development than the gross national product, the percent of work force in agriculture, the percent of population illiterate, etc., because it is based on a nation's wealth rather than on characteristics of its population or production. This indicator also allows us to take

---

[19] As, e.g., the one developed by Bollen (1979).

[20] For a detailed description of the Gini index see Bronfenbrenner (1971).

into account Durkheim's main hypothesis that penal severity decreased with modernization.

Among the most serious problems cross-national research has to cope with is missing data. Due to a lack of available data, the size of the sample is reduced every time a new variable is taken into account. This precludes the study of several possibly influential independent variables. The inclusion of unemployment, e.g., reduced the number of nations for which all other data have been available to merely 21, down from an original sample of 55. To prevent the sample from becoming even smaller, only the variables mentioned here have been analyzed. In an attempt to compromise between sample size and unavailability of data, each independent variable has also been analyzed using all those nations for which it was available, but for which other data were missing.

The data

Data on incarceration rates of 47 nations were taken from a survey conducted by the United Nations in 1975.[21] On eight more countries, data were taken from various sources.[22] As far as possible, data for 1972 were used in order to make the sample as homogenous as possible. Whenever data for 1972 were not available, the year for which they could be obtained was included.

Information on whether a country retains capital punishment or not was taken from the Penal Codes of 23 nations and from a number of international surveys.[23] In partial disagreement with

---

[21] United Nations Working Paper by the Secretariat, Fifth United Nations Congress on Prevention of Crime and Treatment of Offenders (Toronto, Canada, September 1-12, 1975), *The Treatment of the Offender in Custody* and the Community, *with special reference to the application of the standard minimum rules for the treatment of prisoners adopted by the United Nations,* Annex, A/Conf.56/6 (1975).

[22] These sources are: USSR, Indonesia, Hong Kong, South Africa: Eugene Doleschal and Anne Newton, International *Rates of Imprisonment,* Hackensack, N.J.: NCCD, 1981 (unpublished). Poland: Greenberg, 1980. German Democratic Republic: Kaiser, 1976: 39. Yugoslavia: F. Brinc, "Uporaba prostostnih kazni v Francij in Jugoslaviji"(Use of Prison Sentences in France and Yugoslavia), *Revija za Kriminalistiko in Kriminologo* 31: 2 (1980): 102-112; quoted from *Abstracts on Criminology and Penology* 20 (1980): 2909. Switzerland: unpublished survey conducted by the author in 1973.

[23] International surveys on capital punishment: United Nations, Department of Economic and Social Affairs, *Capital* Punishment, (New York: United Nations, 1967); Unite, nations, Economic and Social Council, *Capital Punishment,* (New York: United Nation

some observers (e.g., Lopez-Rey 1980) who even consider a country as retentionist when its laws provide for the death penalty only in times of war, only countries that retain it for normal times and for crimes that are of some relevance during such times[24] were counted as retentionist. No attention was given to whether the death penalty has not been used over a long period of time, as in Belgium or whether executions are quite frequent. The United States, Mexico, an Australia were not included because some of their federal states do retain capital punishment, while others do not.

Regarding the form of government, the necessary information was gathered from the pertinent volumes of the World Almanac[25] Gini index data were taken from an international survey by Bornschier (1978).[26] Since the income distribution within a given nation is extremely stable over even ex tended periods of time,[27] the data used in the present analysis can be considered valid indicators of income concentration in the year for which the incarceration data were obtained. However, to prevent large gaps between incarceration and Gini index data, the analysis has been restricted to countries where the latter are not more than 10 years older than the former.

Data on unemployment rates were taken from the U. N. Statistical Year book, 1978.[28] Wherever possible, data for the year preceding the one for which incarceration rates were available have been gathered.

1973); Amnesty International, *The Death Penalty,* (London: Amnesty International Publications, 1979); Manuel Lopes-Rey (1980).

[24] A good example of a rather theoretical provision for the death penalty is the offense of genocide which, according to the Netherlands Penal Code, is punishable by death.

[25] *The World Almanac and Book of Facts,* (New York: Newspaper Enterprise Association 1972-1981); *Fischer Weltalmanach,* (Frankfurt /Main, FRG: Fischer Verlag, 1972-1981) and the usually more inclusive Fischer Weltalmanach.

[26] Most of these data have been republished in Volker Bornschier and Than-Huye Ballmer-Cao, "Income Inequality: A Cross-National Survey of the Relationship between MNC-Penetration, Dimensions of the Power Structure and Income Distribution,"*American Sociological Review* 44 (June, 1979): 487-506.

[27] See, e.g., the U. S. time-series analysis by Reynolds and Smolensky, 1977.

[28] New York: United Nations, 1979, Table 22.

Data on the per capita national income in 1972, in the year for which incarceration rates were known, have been taken from the pertinent volume of the U. N. Statistical Yearbook.[29] Since changes in per capita national income are affected by fluctuations in exchange rates, and since most incarceration rates were from 1972, all figures were adjusted for dollar rates in 1972.

Results

Capital punishment

As[30] Table 7.1 illustrates,[31] there is a very strong negative association between development (per capita national income) and the retention of capital punishment.[32] Even stronger is, as Table 7.2 reveals,[33] the association between form of government and

---

[29] *U. N. Statistical Yearbook,* 1975, 1977, 1978, (New York: United Nations), for years 1976, 1978, and 1979, (Tables 192, 194, and 193, respectively).

[30] Note that in this paragraph recent developments, such as the abolition of capital punishment in France and in Spain, were taken into account. Therefore, the form of government refers to the present situation, *whereas* it was assessed for the year for which incarceration data were used. Thus, countries such as Portugal and Spain are counted here as democratic, but as non-democratic in connection with incarceration rates. Accordingly, the latest available data on per capita national income have been used here.

[31] The following additional countries have been included:
Nations with at least $1,000 per capita national income (in 1977) without capital punishment: Brazil.
Nations with less than $1,000 per capita national income (in 1977) without capital punishment: Dominican Republic.
Nations with at least $1,000 per capita national income (in 1977) with capital punishment: Bulgaria, CSSR, Greece, Hungary, Iran, Romania, Saudi Arabia.
Nations with less than $1,000 per capita national income (in 1977) with capital punishment: Algeria, Angola Bangladesh, Burma, Cameroon, China (Taiwan), China (PR), Cuba, Egypt, Ethiopia, Ghana, Guatemala, Guinea, Haiti, Madagascar, Malawi, Mali, Mozambique, Niger, Pakistan, Peru, Senegal, South Korea, Sudan, Tanzania, Turkey, Uganda, Upper Volta, Vietnam, Zaire, Zambia, Zimbabwe.

[32] To prevent tiny nations from getting a disproportionate weight, only nations with at least 5 million population have been included. Among those that meet this criterion, four could not be included (Afghanistan, Cambodia, Nepal, North Korea).

[33] The following additional countries have been included: Nations without capital punishment: Brazil, Costa Rica, Uruguay; Nations

retention of the death penalty among the developed nations,[34] i.e. if the level of development is controlled.[35] If no control is introduced, the association is almost perfect (G=.93), since the] are extremely few poor countries with non-democratic forms of government that have abolished capital punishment. The lack of abolitionist countries among developing nations, no matter what the form of government, i.e. the lack of variation in the dependent variable, makes a parallel analysis of the association between form of government and retention vs. abolition of capital punishment among third world nations impossible.

Table 7.1: Capital Punishment and Per Capita National Income
     (Nations with at least 5,000,000 population only)

Capital Punishment	Per Capita National Income		
	Low (<$1,000	High (>$1,000	N
abolished	6%	45%	61
retained	94%	55%	117
N	100% (47)	100% (31)	78

G=-.85* χ^2 =6.37 p<.001

*Note that Gamma should be interpreted with caution, since its amount is due only to the lack of abolitionist countries among the less developed nations. Among the developed ones, there is no parallel tendency.

This lack of variation in the dependent variable, once the level of development is taken into account, makes it also impossible to

---

with capital punishment: Bulgaria, CSSR, Greece, Hungary, Iran, Kuwait, Libya, Romania, Saudi Arabia.

[34] To prevent the sample from becoming too small once control for development is Intl duced, nations having less than 5 but more than 1 million population have been induct in Table 7.2, with the exception of Singapore.

[35] One may question whether Brazil and Uruguay can really be considered abolition countries, in view of the substantial number of non-judicial executions occurring the (Lopez-Rey, 1980; Amnesty International, 1979: 143-146). Not to overstate the case, and to prevent the association from becoming perfect, they were counted here as abolitionist.

analyze the impact of income concentration on whether the death penalty is abolished or retained.[36]

Table 7.2: Capital Punishment and Form of Government
(Nations with at least $1,000 per capita national income in
1977 and 1,000,000 population only)

Capital Punishment	Form of Government		
	Democratic	Non-democratic	N
abolished	76%	17%	22
retained	24%	83%	21
N	100% (25)	100% (18)	43

G=-.88* χ^2 =14.74 p<.001

Incarceration rates[37]

Incarceration rates and development

Although the signs of the zero-order correlation between per capita national income and incarceration rates are in the direction predicted by Durkheim, they are nevertheless very low (r=-.15) far from being significant. For the 54 nations on which data on per capita national income and incarceration could be obtained,

---

[36] Since among wealthy nations mainly communist ones retain capital punishment, and since data on the income concentration there cannot reasonably be used for the present analysis, the variation in the dependent variable is, when Gini index data are used, insufficient among third as well as among first world countries. Overall, i.e. without controlling for development, the association (Gamma) between income concentration (Gini index <.40, .40, -.50, >.50) and abolition vs. retention of capital punishment is .77 (z= 3.15, p<.001, N = 35), but given the strong impact development has on both of these variables, any analysis that does not control for it Is not very meaningful. Besides, Gamma is inflated due to one extreme cell frequency.

[37] A few countries have extremely high incarceration and unemployment rates. Therefore, the analysis has been conducted without these outliers. Since this only increased the correlations between incarceration rate on one hand and Gini index and unemployment on the other hand, but not to any substantial degree, they have been left in the sample.

the zero-order correlation is only -.028. When incarceration rate in these 54 nations is regressed, using per capita national income and form of government simultaneously as independent variables,[38] the β coefficient of the former is far from being significant (t=.90). This finding contrasts sharply with the strong impact that the same indicator of development was found to have on whether capital punishment is retained or abolished (see Table 7.1). Since Newman and Vetere (1978) found a relatively strong correlation (r=.55) between gross domestic product and the number of correctional personnel (per 100,000), one might suspect that the reason for this paradox is that developed and developing countries differ in their control strategies. As prisons are expensive to operate, it seems feasible that countries suffering from scarcity of resources incarcerate fewer people for shorter periods of time than developed nations, and compensate for this lack of deterrence with the use of cheaper but crueler punishment: such as the death penalty. Indeed, there is a surprisingly weak association (G=.26) between capital punishment and incarceration rates.[39] Penal severity, therefore, cannot be regarded as a one dimensional concept. Rather, on should differentiate between two control models that do not necessarily g along with each other, namely a "terror model" aimed at deterrence by cruel punishments, and a "discipline model" that is based on incarcerating more people for longer periods of time. This interpretation can be based on a inversion of Beccaria's famous statement that it is not the cruelty but the certainty of punishment which works as a deterrent, and this is a in line with modern research on the (inverse) relationship between these two variables (cf. Pepinsky, 1980: 82).

Taken together, the relationships found between development on the one hand and capital punishment and incarceration on the other support Durkheim's two laws of penal evolution if they are refined in the following way: (1) Durkheim's hypothesis that penal severity decreases with development, if the dependent variable is operationalized by the shift in the forms of punish-

---

[38] Since the correlation between development and form of government is only -.442, the simultaneous introduction of these two independent variables into the regression equation is not precluded.

[39] Incarceration rates have been categorized as follows: < 5 (N=17), 56-110 (N=19), and >110 (N=15). Gamma (.26) is not significant (z=.78, N=51).

ment, i.e. from capital and corporal to non-physical sanctions, rather than by the severity in sentencing within a given form of punishment; and (2) Durkheim's prediction that imprisonment will become the dominant form of punishment, if it is restated that with development the use of physical form of punishment will decrease. By this refinement, Durkheim's two laws are actually reduced to one.

Incarceration rates and form of government

The zero-order correlation between incarceration rate and form of government is .307 (N=54), and the association coefficient (Gamma) is .16.[40] When incarceration rate is regressed, using per capita national income and form of government as independent variables,[41] the latter's (but not the former's) regression coefficient is significant at the .02 level (t=2.48). In the analysis of variance, form of government explains 11 percent of variation in incarceration rates (N=54) when introduced after the indicator of development. This finding is in line with the result of Table 7.2, although the impact of the form of government on incarceration rates is much smaller than on capital punishment. In line with what has been said above on the impact of development on crime control strategies, it seems that dictatorships are indeed more punitive than other forms of government, for they tend to punish more cruelly instead of incarcerating more people for longer periods of time. This interpretation conforms with Luhmann's (1975: 9) hypothesis that not the use but the threat of force works as a means to maintain power. It is also supported by historical studies on the interaction between terror, i.e. threat with cruel responses, and selective sanctioning practices under the Hanoverian kings (Hay, 1975).

Incarceration rates and income concentration

Among the three independent variables, the Gini index is most strongly correlated with incarceration rates (r=.460).[42] In asses-

---

[40] Incarceration rates have been categorized as follows: <55 (N=17), 56-110 (N=21), and >110 (N=17). Gamma is not significant (s=.47, N=55).

[41] Since the correlation between development and form of government is only -.442, the simultaneous introduction of these two independent variables into the regression equation is not precluded.

[42] Because of the multicolinearity between this variable and per capita national income (r=-.727), a simultaneous multiple regression analysis is not warranted. Stepwise multiple regression, however, is more

sing the causal order among the three independent variables, we can presume that high income concentration and non-democratic forms of government do not cause under-development, but rather that these forms of power concentration are likely to occur at certain stages of development (Bollen, 1979; Bornschier, 1978). Therefore, per capita national income was introduced into the regression equation first. To determine whether form of government or income concentration should be introduced second is somewhat difficult, as highly privileged elites tend to defend the status quo by using dictatorial forms of government; on the other hand, all governments, and non-democratic ones probably even more, try to influence the income distribution by adopting certain economic policies.[43] This stepwise regression analysis revealed that development, once more, does not contribute any substantial fraction to the total amount of variation explained (R^2.023).[44] Since form of government is, as has been discussed above, very strongly associated with retention vs. abolition of capital punishment (see Table 7.2), where income concentration is less strongly associated with the said dependent variable, the results obtained are somewhat puzzling. It seems that non-democratic forms of government and high income inequality go along with the two different crime control strategies described above, the former leading to deterrence by cruel physical punishments, the latter leading to more and longer prison sentences. The rise of democracy during the 19th century was generally followed not only by a marked decline or even the abolition of capital punishment, but also, as Ignatieff (1978: 212) concluded, by the simultaneous massive increase in the use of totalitarian institutions, symbolizing more intolerance towards deviants of all sorts. From these trends, one may say that non-democratic governments prefer the "terror model," whereas democracies with a lot of economic inequality tend to prefer the "discipline model." Whatever the psychological differences underlying these two control models may be, it seems feasible that democratic

---

appropriate whenever an intrinsic causal order among the independent variables can be assumed (Nie et al., 1975: 339).

[43] To avoid any problematic decision in this regard, the analysis was conducted in both ways.

[44] Income concentration was a more powerful explanatory variable (R^2 =.283, p=.001; than form of government, no matter which one was introduced first.

governments are somewhat more restricted in their choice of control strategies, since the use of brutal violence in defense of the status quo can easily destroy the consensual appearance by which such governments tend to be legitimized (cf. Luhmann, 1975: 69). This restriction in the range of available means of control may account for the "economically irrational" reluctance to return to massive execution rates (Rusche, 1933), as well as for the much lower level of police violence against rioters and opponents, when compared to crackdowns under many non-democratic governments. Since using prisons more widely and sentencing offenders to longer prison terms does not seem to be considered illegitimate in democracies, it is plausible that in these countries an increase in penal severity is primarily sought in the form of longer sentences and a more conservative use of non-incarcerative sanctions. Dictatorships however, may depend much less on an image of consensual rule, and this fact allows them to turn to the cheaper "terror model" rather easily, i.e. whenever brutal violence appears to be the most cost-efficient way of defending the status quo.

Incarceration rates and unemployment

Unfortunately, unemployment rates could be obtained for only 21 nations for which data on the other independent variables were available. Thus, the scope of this analysis is very limited.[45] Analyzing the amount of variance explained by each of the independent variables, one may, again, introduce the indicator of development first, since unemployment is obviously a result rather than a cause of underdevelopment. More difficult, however, is the determination of the causal order between unemployment and income concentration. On the one hand, the income concentration index is directly affected by the number of unemployed, since they have less income than people with jobs. To take this mutual dependency into account, the analysis has been conducted both ways, i.e. introducing unemployment before income concentration into the regression equation, as well as the other way around.

Regression analysis revealed that unemployment as well as income concentration explained a substantial amount of variance

---

[45] Again, the high multicolinearity between per capita national income and the Gini index (r=-.707), and between the latter and unemployment (r=.640), renders the use of the simultaneous multiple regression impossible.

in incarceration rates, but both their F-scores reach significance at the .05 level only when introduced before each other. Besides, unemployment seems to be a more powerful variable than income concentration in the present sample.

Before drawing any conclusions regarding the relative import-ance of unemployment and income concentration in explaining incarceration rates, a few words of warning are in order. First, it should be kept in mind that the sample of 21 nations, for which all needed data could be obtained, is heavily biased in favor of affluent countries, the number of countries with less than $1,000 per capita national income being only 4. Since affluent countries have generally quite similar Gini scores, but range very widely in unemployment rates, it is plausible that the latter variable explains more variance within such a restricted sample. Second, in line with this observation, the zero-order correlation between incarceration rate and income concentration is lower (.399) within the sample of 21 nations than within that of 39 nations (.460) which includes 19 developing countries. Unemployment, however, is considerably more strongly correlated with incar-ceration among the 21 nation sample (.546) than if the correlation is computed on the base of 30 nations (.410), i.e. including (mostly developing) countries for which incarceration and unemployment rates, but no data on the other variables, were available.

The data presented here do not warrant any definitive conclusions regarding the overall relevance of unemployment and income concentration in explaining incarceration rates. One may suppose, however, that in relatively poor countries with high inequality of income distribution and endemic high unemployment, the former affects the legitimation of rulers much more seriously than the economic misery which, in the third world, is generally beyond the capacities of those governments to ameliorate drastically. In more affluent nations where the income distribution is more even and, at least in general, less a source of interior conflict, high unemployment rates may have a strong delegitimizing effect, since there are strong expectations that governments have to promote full employment, and that, using the appropriate eco-nomic policies, they could do so. These differences in the de-legitimizing effects of unemployment and income concentration might, then, account for their differential power in explaining incarceration rates, depending on what nations are included in the sample. In the present context, however, this inference should be considered tentative at best.

Discussion

This analysis has yielded a number of empirical relationships. Some of them are in line with the hypotheses presented above, while other findings ask for theoretical integration. Such an integration may be achieved by following a hypothetical model centered around the concept of legitimation crisis, and on the distinction between two different crime control models. Whereas the latter is strongly supported by the data, a few remarks may be in order to make the usefulness of the concept of legitimation more explicit.

Keeping in mind that the present data do indicate that high power concentration, either at the governmental level or in the form of a very unequal income distribution, is associated with more severe punishment, either in the form of capital punishment or longer prison terms, and that unemployment seems to lead to higher incarceration rates, one may question whether it might not have been more appropriate to take these independent variables as causal factors in themselves, instead of using them as indicators of legitimation deficits. Indeed, it seems difficult to operationalize legitimation in theoretical, i.e. prediction-oriented research, although legitimation has been used as a very powerful instrument in all kinds of interpretative, i.e. mainly historical, research.

Faced with such arguments, one could abstain from any attempt at integrating at a more abstract level features of the criminal justice system, such as the disproportionate number of minority and poor persons in prisons, the relationship between unemployment and imprisonment, etc. More frequently, however, such findings are interpreted at a more general level by hypothesizing that the class structure implies attempts by the powerful to "control" the disadvantaged. Although such a proposition may be appealing, it nevertheless fails to state the processes through which power and class conflict may lead to penal severity. Assuming that the powerful have to physically restrain the powerless does not seem very feasible, since such a task would probably exceed the capacities of even the most powerful rulers (cf. Luhmann, 1975: 60-69). More realistically, but still not satisfactory, is the explanation that the criminal law and its sanctions are instruments in the hands of the powerful to deter the disadvantaged from attempting to question the given social structure. Why, then, are waves of repression in many instances directed more at restraining street crime than at cracking down on the opposition, although the former almost never threaten the position of the powerful? And why do incarceration rates fluctuate widely and independently from crime rates?

The concept of legitimation crisis is appealing because it allows the researcher to account for cross-sectional as well as temporal variations in penal severity, which other models fails to explain. Therefore, as operationalization problems arise not only with this concept, but also with many others, it seems preferable to look for more and better indicators than those used here, instead of insisting on less convincing models or, even worse, avoiding entirely the issue of integrating the several features of penal severity.

*This paper was written while the author was a visiting scholar at the School of Criminal Justice, The University at Albany. Thanks are due to Robert Hardt for numerous helpful suggestions concerning the analysis, Graeme Newman for help with data gathering, Beverly Smith for smoothing the paper's English style and Eugene Doleschal, Director, NCCD, for data on incarceration rates and median time served by prisoners.

9. This can't be peace: a pessimist looks at punishment

Harold E. Pepinsky

Punishment doesn't work anymore than following the rainbow leads to a pot of gold. The evidence is all around us. The news is a good place to start.

On this morning's news Britain's unemployment is officially 14 percent, a post-World War II high and still climbing. There has just been rioting again in Liverpool and Brixton. Last winter's letter from a friend in Sheffield reported that fifty percent of teenagers leaving school are unemployed. I recall a special education teacher there in 1983 telling us that her job had become preparing students for lifetime unemployment.

The official British view is that people are losing discipline. If the people only buckled down to work and study, the country could be put back to work. Instead, lower-class rabble are too shiftless to work and too corrupt to earn their living honestly. British victim surveys show that crime is up (Hough and Mayhew, 1985); all good citizens justifiably fear lower-class violence and predation; prison populations continue to mount.

Popular anxiety and anger has foundation. It is not easy for adolescents to keep up the family honor by entering the job market at a respectable level. It is just as hard on parents to wonder whether family security has been achieved for the generation that is coming of age. Understandably, the Prime Minister and her Government want to relieve the fear and anger by venting the heat without bringing down the political order.

This time the Prime Minister's popularity is slipping in the polls. Not for lack of trying. Just as manufacturing an excuse to expel a score of Soviets[1] is harmless compared to sinking the

---

[1] In the late summer of 1985, the person said to be in charge of the KGB in London defected to the British. It turned out that he had been a

Argentinian ship *Belgrano* and ensuing firefights, so rallying to the flag is less noticeable than during the Falklands/Malvinas War. And so far, armed troops haven't been called out against assemblies of "redundant" young Brits. The public hue and cry against foreign or domestic enemies has not been aroused loud enough to justify calling political opposition a threat to national security. Thatcher is in trouble.

On the same news, American unemployment is rising a little from its most recent 7 percent ebb. Black unemployment is back up sharply, but most black teenagers in "the work force" are still holding down jobs.

American police are reporting steadily fewer offenses (FBI). Meanwhile, American punishment of offenders, like the Pentagon budget, is way up. My guess is that long delayed Government figures will eventually show 1985 incarceration rates to be upwards of 350 per 100,000 Americans spending a given day in jail, a juvenile institution or prison; up from 200 per 100,000 in 1974 (Waller and Chan, 1974). If American police crime figures are down, it is because police are busting people for "non-index" public order offenses instead of doing paperwork on behalf of citizen complainants (Pepinsky and Jesilow, 1985: 158-59, 176-77). Drug arrests are really big these days, and down the line, more people do longer jail time.

In some respects, we have gone about as far as we can go. The American Government is disinclined to compile such figures itself, but if you put several of its numbers together, it looks like upwards of 25,000 of every 100,000 black men in their twenties is spending the day in jail or prison, with twice as many on probation and parole (Pepinsky and Jesilow, 1985: 11, 161-62).

Despite drops in police recorded crime, the Government and the media incessantly tell us Americans how much our risk and fear of crime are rising Popular polls run highly in favor of the death penalty and the President. "Red Dawn," the movie about how teenage guerrillas take to Midwestern hills to fight off

---

Western spy for years. Presumably, he could and would have turned in names of Soviet agents in Britain any time the British had demanded it; now the British suddenly "discovered" that a number of Soviet residents somehow worked for the KGB. They and the Soviets went through three months of telling each other's citizens to leave the country. Gullible reporters passed on the lie that spying has suddenly become rampant and more dangerous than ever.

swarms of Soviet paratroopers, vies for popularity with "Miami Vice" on television.

A San Francisco policewoman on the morning news program argues that teenagers are turning to violent caricatures of Satanism because there is so much more "me" than "we" in American families. But such critical insight remains the American exception, rather than the rule. The American rule today is mounting violence against foreign and domestic enemies. Punishment and violence are the national policy of first resort, as indeed they have been since the advent of European settlement (Zinn, 1980).

Some American commentators are telling us that crime is dropping because we have gotten tougher on criminals—that punishment is a force for order and discipline among the population. It helps teach us to refrain from drinking and drugs. Most of all, it teaches our adolescents to purify their bodies and through study of "the basics," to purify their minds as well. Disciplined youth shall diligently search the want ads of their local newspapers and enter, then rise in the job market. Much of this success will be owed to the MX and the prison cell, whose very prospect deters all who would oppose or seek to avoid "free market forces."

Perhaps defenders of the faith in punishing offenders are correct. Perhaps punishment has made Americans relatively secure in their persons or possessions. But if so, then punishment defies every theory of how punishment makes people behave. If punishment works, punishment defies logic. To side with defenders of punishment one must believe in magic.

There isn't much room for optimism about the future course of human events. The logic of a world where the scale of punishment escalates dictates that humanity is headed for self-destruction. Defenders of punishment like Van den Haag (1975), Von Hirsch (1976) and Wilson (1975) have no more reason to hope for a peaceful orderly future than the Jehovah's Witness who stopped by last week to sell "The Watchtower." The strength of their faith in the Revelation that punishment will *save* humanity is admirable.

I'm weaker. I'm skeptical. I'm practically nihilistic. I don't see our world becoming more peaceful and secure unless groups of several hundred people at a time manage to opt out of national governments and multinational corporate economies, which admittedly is a remote prospect.

This essay begins by looking at the impact of wars on crime like those now being waged in Britain and the US. The wars are directed away from the heart of the crime problem, and if established theories of punishment are valid, cause more crime than they prevent. The essay examines why such misdirected wars on crime occur when and where they do. Finally, the essay examines what effective crime control would entail.

What massive punishment accomplishes

There is growing acknowledgment that white-collar crime far, far exceeds street crime (see Ross, 1907; Sutherland, 1940; and recently Reiman, 1984 Pepinsky and Jesilow, 1985). Of course we have only limited estimates of the extent of white-collar crime, but they are enough to make the point For example, the amount Blue Cross/Blue Shield and government medics insurers estimate they lose each year in fraudulent claims, $13 billion, is more than twice the total annual net loss from street crime reported by the FBI This appears to investigators not to be a matter of wholesale fraud by a small number of doctors, but an accumulation of "nickel and diming the system' by most doctors (Pontell et al. 1984). Using the FBI's operating definition of "murder and non-negligent manslaughter" (or as they usually refer to it, just plain "murder"), health care providers appear to claim more than twice the number of victims in hospitals each year as do all police-reported murders combined (Pepinsky and Jesilow, 1985: 60-61, 167).

There is no reason to believe that health care workers are more crooked than other professional groups. The point is that even if one examines narrow band of white-collar activity, there appear to be far more numerous and more serious offenses—both against property and against persons—by people who have attained wealth, power and respectability than by poor young men like those who typically get punished.

It would be surprising if crime were not mostly committed by those at the top of the social order. For one thing, white-collar offenders have power to claim more victims than poor people: they are licensed to put people, to sleep and cut them open; they sell known defective planes or cars to masses of customers; they deal in millions of dollars at a time instead of the occasional television sets, stereos or pocket money. Crime on a grand scale takes less effort the higher one's economic and political position. Indeed because his victim is "remote" the rich and powerful offender may hardly notice committing manslaughter or theft.

For another thing, white-collar offenders have relative immunity from punishment. It is not only that white-collar offenses
are harder to detect and prove than street crimes. The bigger the
crackdown on crime, the more apparent it becomes that officials
are looking for crime in city streets rather than in corporate suites.
The tougher police and courts get on crime, the more apparent it
becomes that the poorer more powerless offenders overwhelm
law enforcement resources. Wars on street crime are a good way
to signal white-collar offenders that the odds of their being caught
and punished for their own offenses are on the decline. *From the
point of view of deterrence theory, one would expect campaigns
against street crime to stimulate white-collar crime, including
corruption of the law enforcers.* Since white-collar crime
contributes the lion's share to overall crime trends and levels, the
net effect of crackdowns on street crime ought to be to increase
victimization by white-collar crime.

As to incapacitating offenders, even imprisonment on today's
grand scale "is like skimming off the tip of an iceberg and telling
ships it is safe to pass" (Pepinsky and Jesilow, 1985: 2). Selective
incapacitation might have at least a transitory impact on overall
victimization if it concentrated on economic and political leaders.
As matters stand, selective incapacitation punishes in proportion
to the length of a police record, which is heavily biased against
identifying more serious crime or criminals. In effect, the commonplace inmate is twice victimized—first by being poor, then
by being picked for punishment not so much for the seriousness
of one's transgressions as for one's powerlessness to resist law
enforcement (Falandysz, 1982; Christie, 1981). Whether police can
clear a substantial percentage of crimes they record by locking up
a few of the people they repeatedly arrest is beside the point, since
the police remain officially unaware of the great bulk of the crime
problem.

To their credit, some defenders of punishment discount punishment's capacity to deter or incapacitate crime and criminals.
Andrew von Hirsch (1976), for example, seeks to be "parsimonious" about justifying punishment by restricting the object to
giving offenders their "just deserts." If in this view punishing
offenders promotes law and order at all, it is because citizens
respect and emulate the moral stance of a government whose
officials inflict due pain on offenders. Citizens obey the laws of
such a government not out of fear, but because they see that the
government is right.

Official campaigns to punish offenders do seem to achieve consensus that those punished are getting no less than they deserve. Brogden (1982) is astonished by the extent of agreement British police achieved this century, from working classes through elites, that underclass young men deserve all the law enforcement they receive. The Communist Manifesto classified common police targets as the "'dangerous class,' the social scum, that passively rotting mass thrown off by the lowest layers of old society..." Americans these days are more likely to say that convicted criminals get off too lightly than that defendants are unfairly treated.

Poland, as reported on recently by a law faculty member from Warsaw (Platek, 1985) is a particularly astounding contemporary case. Its rate of incarceration, circa 400 per 100,000, is higher than the American rate. All but a few hundred of the inmates are prototypic street offenders (Falandysz, 1982). Prison conditions by Western standards are unusually harsh and primitive. The government is extremely unpopular among the citizenry. And yet, according to Platek, Poles generally believe that prisoners have gotten no worse than they deserve, and perhaps deserve worse still.

Platek goes on to describe Poles as a people who have learned that they have to lie, cheat and steal to survive. And who believe that highly placed officials and Party members, and their friends and relatives, are big time crooks. So while popular indignation against the common prison inmate runs high, disrespect for law and government runs even higher.

I have noticed a similar American response, as from students and radio audiences of all political persuasions, to a series of arguments I have made about crime and punishment. When, formerly, I pointed out that street crime might be no worse than thirty years ago for all police figures show, I was castigated for ignoring the plight of victims. When I criticized criminal justice for being ineffectual, I was castigated for being soft on criminals. But when I began instead to point out that white-collar crime was much worse than street crime, audience response warmed considerably. People start in with their own stories and beliefs about crime and corruption in high places. Even if they profess to be law-abiding themselves, they acknowledge that criminality is pervasive.

Former police officer David Toma spoke to the school children of my community several weeks ago, declaring that eighty percent of the children here regularly used illicit drugs; a steady flow of letters to the editor has recently endorsed him for telling it like it is, in a county where expanded drug enforcement has received much publicity.

It is hard if not impossible to quantify cynicism about law and order or overall crime trends, but from Bloomington, Indiana, to Warsaw, Poland, more concerted crackdowns on street offenders do not appear to increase respect for and obedience to law and order. The data may be anecdotal, but the conclusion rests on the theoretical premise that when punishment does not fit the crime, people lose respect for the punishers and for the political and economic elite the punishers represent.

To believe in the effectiveness of just deserts, one would have to suppose that you can fool most of the people most of the time. It is theoretically simpler and cleaner to suppose that people notice punishment depends more on who one is than on what one does. Advocates of fitting the punishment to the crime do not improve on the record of punitive governments. They do not even try to specify how many years of incarceration equals, for instance, the burglary of a certain brand and age of color television set. The classic demonstration that the equation is impossible belongs to Shakespeare, in "Merchant of Venice" (Pepinsky and Jesilow, 1985: 120-30, 170-74).

When people become angry and retributive, it is not because punishments can or do fit crimes, nor because of evidence that people believe it so. Newman's (1983) defense of punishment is especially enlightened in this regard. He simply holds that people punish each other no matter what, not that punishment pays or is morally defensible in the first place. He argues simply that if we are going to punish offenders, we might as well minimize wasteful infliction of pain. He can conceive of no purer punishment than electric shock; certainly, as he argues cogently, electric shock is less painful and wasteful than imprisonment. It is ironic that defenders of imprisonment attack the cold bloodedness of this radically humane and parsimonious defender of punishment.

The question remains why the official urge to punish offenders grows to current British, let alone American, let alone Polish proportions, together with the popular belief that street offenders deserve their punishment. Reasons for such wars on street criminals have nothing to do with fairness or crime prevention. Getting tough on street offenders nonetheless occurs with a certain regularity, which offers explanation if not justification for massive punishment.

Why massive punishment probably happens

Melossi and Pavarini (1981) have traced European and American punishment of offenders through the past several centuries. They note a regularity: Rehabilitation is stressed during periods of full employment; when unemployment rises, officials get tough on their prisoners.

Recent decades in the US illustrate. In the most recent period of prosperity and nearly full employment, the 1960s, incarceration rates declined. They bottomed out in the early 1970s, just as the first of that decade's oil crises led us into what has since become chronic elevated unemployment (for one steady source of incarceration data, see US Dept. of Justice Annual). At the same time, the rhetoric of officials and criminologists shifted from support for rehabilitation toward the view that "nothing works" except purl punishment (heralded, for instance, by Van den Haag, 1975; Von Hirsch 1976; and Wilson, 1975). The appeals for punishment and the ensuing upswing in incarceration is remarkably like American events at the end of the 1920s and through the Depression (Kramer, 1982). Similarly, a resurgence in use of the death penalty has occurred since the latter 1970s, while the previous heyday of capital punishment had been the 1930s.

Another feature of waves of punishing offenders is that they follow within a generation of wars and draw on war rhetoric. American (Selke and Pepinsky, 1982) and British (Critchley, 1978) police launched what they called "war on crime" or a "war against crime" at the time of early post-Work War II recessions, in the latter 1950s. These wars initially took the form of encouraging citizens to report offenses to police, who in turn recorded crimp waves. The police focused public attention on teenage crime at a time when post-War boom babies were just beginning to reach adolescence. Although this campaign to fight young offenders was offset in the 1960s by efforts at "rehabilitation" and "diversion" of offenders, it laid an empirical foundation for the overall punitiveness that began in the mid-1970s.

Criminologists have drawn a contrast between the fear and punishment in the United States in the mid-1970s, and the relative calm sense of having little crime, lack of resort to arrest and incarceration, keeping prison terms short and avoiding officially supervised probation in Japan (Clifford 1976) and Switzerland

(Clinard, 1978). One of these countries, Japan, hat been pacified as a loser of World War II, and the other, Switzerland, has been neutral. It is not necessarily the case that crime itself was low in these countries.[2] *Concern* about crime was low, and punishment of offenders sparing. In particular, adult-youth relations seemed relatively secure, in economies that were still expanding and rapidly hiring citizens who were of age to enter the work force.

Costa Rica (Montero, 1983; Busey, 1962) is another country which fit the pattern at least into the beginning of the 1980s. Its incarceration rate remained low; not much effort was expended on law enforcement. Costa Rica had been neutral during World War II. The major government expenditure was in opening civil service jobs for children of the middle class, whose economic and political future appeared guaranteed.

Non-punitive times for these "crime-free" countries may be changing. Economic opportunities for youth, for example apprenticeships in Switzerland, seem to be shrinking, and alarm about youth, as over violence in Japanese schools, seems to be increasing. The pressure of Costa Rica's foreign debt and military involvement with the US may have begun to change the economy and politics of punishment there. But while the boom times lasted, to criminologists these countries were models of how to succeed in not having to punish street offenders.

The timing and focus of waves of punishing street offenders are suggestive. The legitimacy of punitive governments seems to have rested on military prowess, demonstrated in recent wars. Attention in punitive societies appears focused on the indiscipline of adolescents, at a time when unemployment is rising and hence prospects for entry into the job market are diminishing. The threat of disorder is real. The threat is not so much that unemployed people commit crime, but that the honor and welfare of families throughout the social order will not be sustained into the next generation. Poor young men just happen to be a politically convenient, tangible target for fear and anxiety over much broader problems.

Campaigns to punish street offenders worsen the problem. The policy encourages crime at the top of the social order, as we have seen, making people more vulnerable to violence and predation

---

[2] See, for instance, Ziegler's (1979) attempt to demonstrate that crime and corruption are rampant among the *Swiss* political and economic elite.

than ever. In a larger sense, wars on foreign enemies and on domestic street offenders alike are inherently destabilizing. They make job prospects for coming generations less secure. The United States is a poignant example (Zinn, 1980): Wars have alternated with crackdowns on poor citizens within our communities. To be sure, an incredible share of the world's wealth has been captured and drawn into the country; the average American is by world standards quite rich. But from the killing and removal of American Indians onward, the scale of violence in which we have participated has escalated—now alternating between global warfare against foreign enemies and punishment of record proportions of our own population as criminals. For a century and one half, not a decade has passed without foreign wars or crises of domestic disorder. Today's rampant fear of foreign and domestic enemies is nothing new for Americans, but it has not abated either.

It is equally counterproductive to lay blame for crime and punishment on groups other than street offenders (see Galtung, 1969). Ranulf (1964, originally 1938 in Danish), for example, tried blaming the "moral indignation" underlying wars on crime on political dominance by lower middle classes. This erudite study is essentially an attack on Nazism, backed up by a series of historical case studies of other times and places. The apparent message: Nazi supporters are too uncultured and unrefined to be politically fair and decent. As Harold Lasswell points out in the preface to the English edition of the book (Ranulf, 1964: ix-xiii), Ranulf overlooks how convenient punitive politics are to economic elites—whose support for punishment is no less important for being subdued.

It is more commonplace to blame elites for crime and punishment. The profit most from crime and punishment, to be sure. Their resistance to economic and political restructuring is most potent, obviously. The problem is that removing and punishing elites relieves crime and punishment more than temporarily, and at a cost. Political revolution creates the same problems it aims to solve. China is a noteworthy contemporary example. The worst criminals were thrown out of power in the course and immediate aftermath of the 1949 revolution. But now that post-revolutionary babies are moving into adulthood, they confront an entrenched, often crooked and punitive new elite of revolutionaries. The faces at the top have changed, but the fact of exploitation and violence led from the top has quickly reemerge in the new political order.

Mao Zedong may have hoped that elites would continue to be punished for their transgressions and removed in a process "continuing revolution," but instead the revolution itself became corrupted (Pepinsky, 1982). Since tens of thousands of offenders have apparently been executed in China the last couple of years, it is hard to say that punishing rich and powerful offenders rather than concentrating on poor street offenders has led the country to freedom from economic insecurity and attendant crime and punishment (Schell, 1984; Tifft, 1985).

Political revolutions strip away the pretense that those who uphold law' with violence are any more virtuous or less harmful than those who break law' with violence. They also help make it apparent that governments' "punishments" and offenders' "crimes" are essentially like response to like behavior, each feeds upon and amplifies the other even when the criminal class becomes the government. No matter who gets punished, punishment ends up making crime worse.

It may be that punishment is necessary, and that worse crime problem require more punishment. If so, crime and violence and social insecurity have no way to go but up. If so, crime and injustice have to escalate. Escalation cannot continue much longer before our species obliterates itself. Defenders of punishment have no empirical foundation for believing otherwise. A belief that punishment can "work" is the height of unwarranted optimism about the human condition.

Some criminologists, including me, are pessimistic enough to believe that relief from crime is much harder, much less likely, than any form of tinkering with punishment can possibly achieve.

The only way out

Relief from crime requires relief from the urge to punish. Relief from the urge to punish requires confidence among parental generations that the generations corning into adulthood will attain positions of honor and economic security. The confidence cannot be achieved through punishment or other violence. That is, those who gain such confidence and security cannot do it at the expense of others. This is not moral rhetoric; it is simple political reality.

Some criminologists are beginning to pinpoint *necessary* conditions for such human development. (Who could even dream of *sufficient* conditions for freedom from crime, violence and injustice?)

The essential requirement is this: Non-punitive people must foresee that they (let alone the next generation) gain by giving power to some of those who would otherwise offend them (see e.g., Tifft and Sullivan, 1980) and ignoring the rest (Felstiner, 1974). This requirement is commonly known as "anarchism." Anarchism is not enough.

In a violent, capricious world, foreseeing that one gains without punishment requires elaborate guarantees that people one depends upon will not gain at one's expense. Anthropologists call these guarantees "cross-cutting ties" (Nader and Parnell, 1983: 204); Christie (1981: 88-89) calls them "mutual dependence." They are a complex balance of reciprocal rights and duties which work only when elaborately organized, as in the constitutions of the 150 successful Mondragon enterprises in Basque Spain, which guarantee open entry for would-be worker owners and their descendants (Oakeshott, 1978; Henk and Logan, 1982; Gutierrez-Johnson, 1984). People who feel a stake in disputes must see that they "own" or can substantially affect outcomes (Christic, 1977); those who would sit in judgment on others must feel "vulnerable" to the accused (Christie, 1981: 81-83). All in all, those who would refrain from ratifying or executing punishment must have intimate "knowledge" of people upon whom their economic well-being appears to depend (Christie, 1981: 85-88). In other words, the free flow of information—known in legal parlance as accountability and standing to be heard—must be guaranteed for people to refrain from punishment and contain crime and violence (Wilkins, 1984; Pepinsky, 1986).

Certain reporters see such communities of interest beyond punishment being created, either before conflicts emerge (as in the magazine *Changing Work,* 1984) or in reconciliation of conflicts thereafter (as in victim-offender reconciliation programs; Imma-rigeon, 1984). Insofar as such efforts succeed they must be:

a. Meticulously, painstakingly constituted, not so much as to who gets what, as instead to *who gets to decide* who gets what. Constituting peaceful groups demands a political science or legal skill of incredible detail and precision.

b. Planned for no more than several hundred people at a time, perhaps in limited networks. Human intelligence cannot hear members of larger communities well enough to plan without doing systematic violence to some groups, and as a consequence, generating upward spirals of crime and punishment.

c. Relatively obscure. Information can be shared about successes in developing peaceful communities, but if a single community gains prominence, political and economic elites around it can be expected to suppress it. Social movement beyond punishment and crime has to occur in the little social spaces which escape the attention of economic and political establishments.

The more realistic relief from crime and punishment is, the more improbable it becomes. It is tempting to conclude that since life beyond punishment is so improbable, punishment must be planned as best we can. But no matte] how carefully punishment gets planned, it makes crime and violence worse The more grand the plan, the worse the result. You will find that criminologists who try to find ways to transcend punishment and crime have a pretty bleak outlook on the future of humankind. They just don't see any point in deceiving ourselves that crime can in any way be controlled on a grand and violent scale. No matter how improbable, they try to content themselves with the possible. Hope for improvement of the human condition may not have much foundation, but that is no excuse for the blind optimism of the utopian criminologists who believe that punishment can work.

10. Punishment and social structure: what does the future hold?

Thomas J. Bernard

What will punishment be like in the future? Will the amount of punishment increase or decrease? Will imprisonment remain a major form of punishment, or will it be replaced by community treatments or corporal punishments? Will punishments become more oriented to restitution and less to vengeance, or vice versa?

These and other questions about the future of punishment are especially interesting when considered in the long run. Long-range projections about the future of punishment would have to consider the kinds of fundamental social structural changes that occur in societies over time. For example, the "industrial revolution" occurred in Western societies at a particular point in time (Foucault, 1977). This revolution was associated with enormous changes in social structural arrangements, so that rural, agricultural, aristocratic, and feudalistic societies were transformed into urban, industrial, democratic, and capitalistic societies. While there is controversy about the specifics, it is clear that these changes in social structure were associated with enormous changes in the nature and extent of punishments (Foucault, 1977; Shelley, 1981). Longer range projections about the future of punishment would have to consider the possibility that such fundamental social structural changes would again occur in societies, changes which could again transform the nature of punishments.

This chapter looks at the future of punishment within the context of broader social and historical changes. This is an inherently speculative enterprise, since the only way to know for sure what the future holds is to wait for it to get here. Nevertheless, it is possible to analyze major trends that have occurred in past societies, and use that analysis to project trends that are likely to occur in future societies.

A number of theorists have constructed their theories in precisely this way (Nisbet, 1966: 71-82). This chapter uses three of those theorists–Marx, Durkheim, and Simmel—as guides to speculate on the nature and extent of punishment in the future. These theorists are chosen because the: represent three quite different traditions within the sociological framework (Bernard, 1983). Most sociologists and criminologists view the world within a framework that, to some extent at least, originates with one or another of these theorists. To the extent that sociologists and criminologists speculate on the future of punishment, they do so within the context of assumption similar to the ones held by these theorists. Thus, looking at the future of punishment within the context of these three theories gives us a sense of the range of ideas on the subject.

Projections on the future of punishment must be done in the context and broader projections about the future of societies generally. Thus, for each of the three theorists, the chapter presents a brief overview of how they analyzed the past development of societies, and how they thought that development would continue in the future. The nature and extent of punishment within those future societies is then discussed.

Durkheim

Like other social theorists of his time, Durkheim used the analysis of pas trends to project future developments in his own and other contemporary societies. One aspect of this analysis involved projections about future developments concerning criminal punishments. A brief description of his genera theory of social development is presented, and then the discussion focuses specifically on its implications for the nature and extent of punishments in future societies.

Durkheim's theory was phrased in terms of the inevitable historical development of society from a primitive stage to an advanced one (Durkheim 1965). In the primitive, "mechanical" form of society, each social group is relatively isolated from other groups and is basically self-sufficient. Within these social groups, individuals live under largely identical circumstances, do identical work, and hold identical values. There is little division of labor, with only a few persons in the clan or village having specialized functions. In contrast, the advanced, "organic" form of society has a highly developed division of labor, and social solidarity is based on the diversity of functions of the different parts of the society. Durkheim argued that all societies were at some stage of progression between the mechanical and the organic forms, with none being totally one or the other.

Law and punishment take very different forms in those societies. In mechanical societies, social solidarity arises from pressure for uniformity exerted against the inevitable diversity of its members. Such pressure is exerted in varying forms and degrees. In its strongest form, it consists of criminal punishments.

These punishments, according to Durkheim, are one of the most fundamental means by which social solidarity is maintained. Law is oriented toward repressing deviation from the norms of the time, but the norms are defined in such a way that it is inevitable that a certain portion of the population will fail to live up to them. Individuals who violate norms are punished as a means of expressing the moral superiority and group solidarity of the norm-abiding citizens, rather than for deterrence or retributive purposes. Essentially, the punishment of criminals bonds the law-abiding members of society into a coherent group. Such punishment therefore serves socially useful functions, independent of its effect on criminal behavior. Durkheim therefore argued that punishment is "normal" in mechanical societies—i.e., it will be found in all societies independent of the behavior of the members of the society.

As the society progresses towards the organic state, however, the role for punishment changes. Solidarity more and more is based on the diversity of functions of its members, rather than on their uniformity. Law regulates the interactions among the different parts of the society, and punishment is one means of providing restitution in the case of wrongful transactions.

Durkheim believed that hierarchy was inevitable in every society, and thus it would also be found in all future societies. However, he argued that hierarchy itself was not a cause of social maladies since it reflected basic inequalities in human nature (Taylor et al. 1973: 67-90). Criminal and other deviant behaviors were said to emerge when individuals occupied social positions in the hierarchy that were inappropriate to their natural abilities.

One of the most important aspects of Durkheim's future society therefore was that individuals had to be free to rise or fall to their proper place society in a "spontaneous" division of labor (Taylor et al., 973: 74-78).

Durkheim also recommended the establishment of a network of professional and occupational groups that would act as buffers between the individual and the state (1964: 1-38; 1951: 373-86). These groups would alias full communication between the state and all of the various subgroups within it. Out of this mechanism would come a society in which individuals and groups received an appropriate portion of the goods of society, in proportion to their talents and abilities. As a result, all these individuals would be adequately bonded to society, and there would be a minimum of deviant behaviors such as crime.

Durkheim maintained that the organic society was not merely an idea but was also "normal" in the sense that all societies were tending to evolve into this state through the normal processes of social development. The state of Durkheim's own society, which he described as filled with enormous amounts of conflict and unfairness, was said to be a temporary aberration resulting from the French and Industrial Revolutions. On the basis of Durkheim's general theory of social development, as we, as his specific arguments about the functions of punishment, we can project that, as societies evolve toward the organic state over the long period of time, there will be a steady decline in the types of behaviors usually described as crime. As mobility increases and individuals and groups assume their rightful places within the social structure, fewer people occupy inappropriate social structural locations. Accordingly, there will be fewer deviant behaviors. At the same time, there will also be a decline in the social need for punishment, since those arise from the pressures for conformity exerted against human diversity, generating feelings of solidarity in mechanical societies. As societies advance more toward the organic state, this becomes less and less important as a source of solidarity. Thus, the future society will according to Durkheim, contain fewer and fewer truly "deviant" behaviors and at the same time have an increasing tolerance and acceptance of-human diversity.

In essence, Durkheim's theory projects a society in which the criminal law, with its emphasis on retributive punishment, simply fades from the scene. What remains is essentially civil law, in which individuals file grievances against each other over allegations of unfair transactions. Those grievances are presented before the neutral state, which metes out punishments in the form of restitutive sanctions against the offending party. Some years ago, Taylor et al. (1973: 282) issues a clarion call to "create a society in which the facts of human diversity, whether personal, organic or social, are not subject to the power to criminalize." According to Durkheim, such a society will be the inevitable and normal outcome of ongoing processes of social development.

This is an attractive future to be sure, especially since Durkheim argued that it is not only inevitable but that it will be achieved in the normal course of the evolutionary development of present societies. There are many questions that can be raised about this scenario, but a few will suffice for the present chapter. First, this scenario assumes that social hierarchy is inevitable. Others, however, have argued that nonhierarchical societies have existed in the past and are possible in the present and future (e.g., Pfohl, 1985: 28-29; 351-53). Second, even if one agrees that hierarchy is inevitable in every society, one could still disagree with Durkheim's argument that individuals at their "proper place" according to their native abilities will be adequately bonded to society. It may well be that individuals at the bottom of the social hierarchy will be dissatisfied with their place in society, even if they perceive themselves to have the least talents and abilities (see Bernard, 1984; Vold and Bernard, 1986: 202-03). This dissatisfaction would deregulate the natural drives, allowing people to want more than they have within the structure of society. These individuals would then have a tendency to engage in criminal and deviant behaviors.

Durkheim's projections about the future of punishment make sense only if one assumes, as he did, that social hierarchy is inevitable and that individuals on the bottom of the social hierarchy will be adequately bonded to society so long as their status reflects their natural abilities. Many contemporary criminologists and sociologists do hold these assumptions. They therefore expect contemporary societies to evolve in the direction of fuller mobility and a "spontaneous" division of labor. Associated with this general pattern of social development would be a long-term decline in the types of behaviors requiring punishments, as well as a long-term decline in social needs to punish individuals regardless of their behaviors. A very different view of the future, however, it held by sociologists and criminologists who hold Marxist rather than Durkheimian assumptions.

Karl Marx

Karl Marx made very different assumptions about social hierarchy than did Durkheim. He believed that hierarchy was characteristic of the present stage of social development but that it did not exist in at least some past stage and would not exist in future stages. He also argued that individuals at the bottom of the social hierarchy would be alienated from society and would suffer from a wide range of social problems even if their social position was "appropriate," given their talents. Like Durkheim, Marx constructed hi theory by analyzing past trends and used them to project future developments. This general analysis will be presented first, and then the discussion will shift to specific implications about punishment in future societies.

Marx's (1967, 1970a) theory was essentially an economic interpretation of history, rather than a theory of individual or group behavior. The principal conflict that Marx presented, and on which his theory is based, was the conflict between the material forces of production and social relations of production. The material forces of production can generally be considered to be society's capacity to produce, which includes both technological equipment and the knowledge, skill, and organization to use that equipment. The social relations of production refer primarily to property relations, and consequently to the distribution of income generated by the material force of production.

The development of the material forces of production is relatively continuous throughout history, whereas the social relations of production tend to freeze into particular patterns. Social relations tend to change only abrupt: and violently in revolutions when they have become so inconsistent with the material forces that they substantially impede the further development of production. Thus, for example, the social relations of feudalism gave way to bourgeois capitalism with the advent of industrialized society. The social relations of capitalism initially acted as a stimulant to industrial production but, Marx argued, were becoming an impediment to the further development of the material forces of production due to certain inherent contradiction in the capitalist system.

In particular, Marx argued that the system would inevitably concentrate the ownership of the means of production into fewer and fewer hands. Because of increasing mechanization, there would also be a growing pool of unemployed and underemployed workers, and those workers who were employed would be paid subsistence wages because of the labor surplus and the competition for jobs. Thus, the capitalist system would inevitably tend toward a polarization of society into two classes, one of which was both shrinking and becoming grotesquely wealthy and the other of which was large, growing, and barely able to survive.

Here the contradiction between the forces of production and the relations of production is quite clear, as is the necessity for a revolutionary restructuring of the relations of production. That restructuring would consist, according to Marx, of establishing collective ownership of the means of production and instituting centralized planning to end the cycles of overproduction and depression that plagued capitalism. It would also mean the end of classes and class conflict, and the establishment of a non-antagonistic society.

Marx believed that individuals on the bottom of this social hierarchy would be afflicted by a variety of problems regardless of whether their social status was "appropriate" for their natural abilities. Specifically, he argued that it was essential for human nature that people be productive in life and in work (Hirst, 1975). But in capitalist societies, there are large number of unemployed and underemployed people who are maintained in their status to meet the shifting labor and consumption needs of industry. These people become "demoralized" due to their lack of productivity and are therefore susceptible to all forms of crime and vice. Marx called these people the "lumpen proletariat."

Criminal punishments serve two purposes in capitalist societies, according to Marx. First, punishments responded to the criminal behaviors of the lumpen proletariat. Those behaviors, of course, were generated by the social conditions of capitalism, but Marx described them as genuinely criminal so that other groups, particularly the working class, required protection against them. Second, criminal punishments were also used by the ruling class as one of many tools by which they maintained control over the other groups in society, particularly with respect to exploiting those groups in pursuit of their own economic interests.

Marx did not describe in detail the nature of the non-antagonistic society that would emerge with the advent of communism. But he did provide some general information about it in the *Critique of the Gotha Programme* (1970b). Initially, the proletariat would have to defend itself against its enemies by assuming dictatorial control of the state mechanisms. But as full communism developed, the proletariat would form the "immense majority" of the population, and their enemies would become fewer and fewer. The state itself would then begin to wither away, and men would cease to govern men but would only administer things. There would be no exploited class who would want to revolt and no state to revolt against.

Marx did not argue that communism would be characterized by a total absence of conflict. The normal conflicts between individuals and groups would continue in that society as in any other. However, communist society would be free from basic structural conflicts that generate fundamental social change. Thus, normal conflicts between individuals and groups would occur within the context of a stable social structure.

Despite the fact that Marx did not describe communist society as to tally conflict free, he expected that the level of conflict within it would decrease dramatically because conflicts were attributed to social structural arrangements, not to human nature. Once those social structural arrangements were changed, it was reasonable to expect that the conflicts themselves would disappear (Bernard, 1983). That would include the "street" crime of the lumpen proletariat, as well as the "white collar crimes" of the ruling class, such as economic exploitation, hazardous working conditions, toxic environmental pollution, unemployment and underemployment, etc.

Criminologists and sociologists who hold Marxist assumptions see the future of punishment in similar terms. They believe that the evolutionary development of capitalist societies is in the direction of increased crisis. Ai long as that crisis deepens, they expect to see expanding use of criminal punishment. In part, this will result from a rising tide of criminal behaviors by the lumpen proletariat, who both will grow in numbers and becoming increasingly demoralized due to the deepening crisis of their social conditions. In part, this will result from the deepening crisis itself, as the ruling class uses criminal punishments in their (ultimately futile) attempt to stamp out opposition. The crisis, however, can only terminate in a revolutionary overthrow of the capitalist economic system and the establishment of socialism. Once that event takes place, Marxist sociologists and criminologists expect to see a rather rapid long-term decline in criminal punishments, due to a decline both in criminal behaviors and a decline in the need to repress segments of the population. This will culminate in a society in which the behaviors typically subjected to criminal punishments, as well as the criminal punishments themselves, are infrequent to nonexistent.

Simmel

A third classical theorist who has had a major impact on contemporary sociology and criminology is Georg Simmel.

Unlike Durkheim and Marx, Simmel did not display an overriding interest in the historical process of social development, although he did describe a general pattern by which societies developed. His focus was more directly on understanding and describing existing societies. He argued that conflict was an inevitable and necessary part of every society, and he did not argue that there was a natural pattern of social development that would result in a society that had a minimal level of conflict. Simmel's theory did contain implications about social structural conditions under which the negative effects of conflicts could be minimized, but he did not argue that there was a broad historical trend towards the development of these conditions in contemporary societies. To that extent, Simmel's theory was considerably more pessimistic than either Durkheim's or Marx's.

Simmel (1950) held that "society" consists of the set of all reciprocal relationships between individuals. These relationships could be as simple as "two people who for a moment look at one another or who collide in front of a ticket window," or as enduring as a life-long marriage. In general, Simmel reserved the term "society" to describe the set of permanent patterns of social interaction. These permanent patterns are taken to define the groups or social circles to which the person belongs (Simmel, 1955). The largest of these groups is the state, but in modern society an individual may belong to a wide variety of different groups, having different roles and statuses in each of them.

The extent to which a group is tightly knit can be gauged by the extent to which it has a "code of honor" regulating the behavior of its members. Individuals are frequently affiliated with groups that have conflicting codes on specific issues or that represent interests that are opposed to each other. But Simmel identified membership in groups having conflicting values or interests with the growth of human freedom and individuality. Simmel argued that groups are initially formed on the basis of propinquity (such as the family and the local community), but that later associations tend to be formed on the basis of "common interests." Here, Simmel used the term "interest" in the broadest sense of having an interest in or being interested in a common purpose. That included, but by no means was limited to, economic interests.

The development from groups based on propinquity to groups based on common interests is characteristic of both individuals and society in general. This development is associated with the growth of human freedom because the second type of group formation is a matter of choice, while the first is not. It is also associated with the development of individuality because one's identity or personality is ultimately rooted in the groups to which one belongs. In primitive cultures, and for young human beings, only one group exists, and one's identity is drawn entirely from that group. But when one belongs to several groups that are in conflict among themselves, me must resolve those conflicts in terms of the uniqueness of the self. That is, one gains freedom and individuality as one becomes associated with a multiplicity of conflicting groups.

It was in this context that Simmel argued that conflict was an essential part of the unity of societies. Societies are not "less" societies because they contain conflicts—rather, the conflicts they contain are an integral part of the society itself. These conflicts have a variety of consequences. Some of these consequences are positive or beneficial, such as contributing to the growth of freedom and individuality. Other consequences, however, are negative and harmful. Crime and punishment are two of the negative consequences of conflict.

Simmel (1959) argued that the proper subject of sociological inquiry were the "forms" of social interaction, but not the "content." Content included everything that might be thought of as the "causes" of conflictual behavior—drive, interest, purpose, inclination, psychic state, movement. These "motivations" are not in themselves social and are not the subject to sociological inquiry. Simmel simply presumed that these motivations exist, have always existed, and will always exist. According to Simmel, sociological inquiry properly focuses on the forms through which these motivations are expressed. Conflict is an inevitable and necessary form of social interaction because these motivations inevitably and necessarily exist.

Simmel's analysis of the causes or sources of conflict was quite limited since he considered this part of the "content" of conflict and thus not the proper subject matter of sociology. He did make general statements about "hostile impulses" and "needs for hating and fighting" that would seem to locate the causes of at least some conflicts in human nature. However, Simmel (1950: 34-35) also stated that the only case of conflict that can be explained solely by psychological motivations is an antagonistic game in which there is no prize for winning. Thus, the major source of conflict within his theory seems to be "conflicts of interest" rooted in social structural arrangements.

Coser (1956:55-60) elaborated on Simmel's argument, maintaining that hostile impulses and real conflicts over interests are separate phenomena Conflicts over interests frequently occur without any hostility between participants, and conflicts involving hostile impulses frequently do not involve pursuit of any interests. Along with Simmel, he pointed out that it may be "useful" to hate an enemy, but that such hatred is generally secondary to the concrete sources of the conflict that lie in conflicting interests. Dahrendorf (1959) similarly assumes a conflictual human nature as the source of at least some conflicts, but he focuses exclusively on structural conflicts of interest as a source of violence. His recommendations for reducing the violence associated with conflicts entail social structural reforms.

While Simmel did not present an overall theory of the historical processes of social development, he did describe a general tendency through which societies increasingly differentiate into greater numbers and varieties of interest groups, allowing ever great freedom and individuality. To the extent that an ideal society appears in Simmel's theory, it is a society in which the process of differentiation into conflicting interest groups is highly advanced, so that the maximum potential for individualization and freedom are achieved.

Conflict will be present even in this ideal society since conflict is an integral part of every society. The implication of that view is that conflict is not a problem that can be "solved," but it is a continuing presence in society that can only be "managed" in an effort to reduce its negative consequences. Simmel's theory contains a number of implications about the social conditions under which the negative consequences of conflicts, including crimes and punishments, can be reduced. These implications have been presented in more detail by Dahrendorf, relying primarily on Simmel's formulations.

Dahrendorf denies that conflict can be suppressed over any considerable length of time, and also denies that societies are possible in which conflicts are actually resolved. However, he (1959: 225-27) argues that conflicts can be "regulated" in a society so as to reduce the level of violence associated with them. There are three prerequisites for the effective regulation of conflict. The first is the recognition that one is in a conflict situation by acknowledging that the opponent has the right to make a case. That is to be distinguished from acknowledging that the case one's opponents is making is "right." The second prerequisite is the formation of interest groups. Simmel and Coser argue that it is only by providing organized channels for the expression of grievances and hostilities that social life is able to continue. Without such channels, relationships between antagonistic groups would sunder. The third is the evolution of certain "rules of the game" that can provide a formal framework for the relations between the conflicting parties. The presence of these three prerequisites does not guarantee that conflict will be regulated, but Dahrendorf argues that regulation is impossible without them.

This process is similar to what Durkheim described as the evolution of regulations in organic societies. Dahrendorf, however, pointed out that different groups participate in the process of forming these rules to different degrees. To the extent that a group participates in the process of forming the rules, the regulation of conflict will be effective, since they develop legitimate channels to pursue their values and interests, as well as to express their hostilities and grievances. For groups that do not participate, the process does not provide similar channels, so that conflicts tend to be unregulated. Unregulated conflicts are generally expressed in more violent ways, and arc defined as crime and other forms of social deviance.

This suggests that for processes of conflict regulation to work effectively there must be some redistribution of power in society. More powerful group: in society must recognize that less powerful groups have a case to make These less powerful groups must be allowed to form interest groups to pursue their case, and rules for interaction must be worked out between the more powerful and less powerful groups. The rules already worked out for interaction among the more-powerful groups cannot simply be applied to the less-powerful groups.

One method for encouraging the formation of interest groups by less powerful segments of the population is by funding agencies whose purpose is to pursue and defend the values and interests of those segments. For example, Rose (1972) argues that Community Action Agencies were designed in part to represent the values and interests of poor people in the political arena. He also argues that they failed in this purpose because they were taken over by the existing community social services agencies and used to promote their own institutional values and interests.

Future developments in punishment, within the context of Simmel's theory, will be determined by the nature of social structural arrangements particularly with respect to whether or not they allow for the regulation of conflict. To a considerable extent, that depends on whether power is closely held by more powerful groups to the exclusion of the less powerful or whether there is some redistribution of power so that the less powerful are able to genuinely pursue their interests, defend their values, and redress their grievances against more powerful groups. Under those conditions, conflicts between groups will still remain, but the negative consequences of conflicts, including crimes and punishments, will be minimized. Simmel does not maintain that there is a clearly defined historical process through which societies will inevitably develop into these more peaceable states. Thus, unlike Durkheim and Marx, Simmel does not project an inevitable historical development that ends in a low level of criminal punishments.

Conclusion

The implications about the future of punishment that are found in Simmel's theory bear some resemblance to the implications that are found in both Durkheim and Marx. On the one hand, Simmel's theory implies the need for social structural reforms that entail a redistribution of power. This is similar to the policy implications found in Marx's theory. The differences between the two theories are that Simmel makes no explicit connection between the redistribution of power and ownership of the means of production, and he does not view this change as part of an inevitable historical process. To some extent, Marx's theory can be viewed as a specific historical argument that can be encompassed within the framework of Simmel's general ahistorical argument.

On the other hand, Simmel's theory implies that negative consequences of conflict, such as crime and punishment, can be reduced if the isolated individual is bonded to a group that will represent his values and interests while interacting with other groups according to mutually-agreed upon rules. That bears considerable resemblance to the implications of Durkheim's theory, which recommends the bonding of the individual to a network of professional and occupational groups in the development of "organic" solidarity. Simmel's theory suggests, however, that these groups do not presently exist or powerless people, and that their development would challenge the values and interests of the more powerful groups who would therefore oppose them. Thus, in contrast to Durkheim's, Simmel's theory does not suggest that there is an inevitable historical process by which punishments will be reduced.

Durkheim also argued that social solidarity is derived in part from the labeling and expulsion of "deviants." Within the context of Simmel's theory, this process is described as the integration of a very large conflict group (the dominant group within society) on the basis of conflict with a very small, generally disorganized group (deviants). Durkheim argued that in the natural course of social development, the societal need to label and expel deviants would diminish and be replaced by an increasing acceptance of diversity. That optimistic projection is not matched by a similar argument in Simmel's theory. Simmel, in contrast, describes the need to generate internal enemies as a deeply rooted social psychological reality in every society. It is perhaps as deeply rooted as the need to generate external enemies through war and threats of war (James, 1910), both being manifestations of what Simmel called the "inborn needs for hating and fighting." The formation of interest groups among less powerful portions of the population would directly contradict the social psychological need to define some groups in society as "deviants" who do not have the "right to make a case." Whether it is possible to have a society without "deviants" is not at all clear.

References

Abbott, Andrew. 1983. "Professional ethics," *American Journal of Sociology* 88: 855-885.

Alexander, Charles P. 1985. "Crime in the Suites," *Time,* 10 June, 52-53.

American Bar Association. 1980. *Standards for Criminal Justice.* Vol.3 Boston: Little, Brown.

Amnesty International. 1979. *The Death Penalty.* London: Amnesty International Publications.

Andenaes, Johannes. 1971. "The moral or educative influence of criminal law." Journal *of Social Issues* 27: 17-31.

Andenaes, Johannes. 1975. "General prevention revisited: research and policy implications," *The Journal of Criminal Law and Criminology* 66 338-365.

Australia Trade Practices Commission. 1978. *Fourth Annual Report, Yea, Ended 30th June 1978.* Canberra: Australian Government Publishing Service.

Aydelotte, F. *1913.Elizabethan Rogues and Vagabonds.* Oxford: Clarendon Press.

Ball, Harry V. and Lawrence M. Friedman. 1968. "The Use of Criminal Sanctions in the Enforcement of Economic Legislation: A Sociological View," in *White-Collar Criminal.* ed. Gilbert Geis. New York: Atherton pp. 410-432.

Banfield, Edward C. 1970. *The Unheavenly City.* Boston: Little, Brown and Co.

Bardach, E., and R.A. Kagan. 1982. *Going by the Book: The Problem of Regulatory Unreasonableness.* Philadelphia: Temple U. Press.

Barrett, A.R. 1895. *The Era of Fraud and Embezzlement.* Boston: Publisher unknown.

Becker, H. 1963. *Outsiders: Studies in the Sociology of Deviance.* London: Collier-Macmillan.

Bernard, T.J. 1983. *The Consensus-Conflict Debate.* New York: Columbia.

Bernard, T.J. 1984. "Control Criticisms of Strain Theories," *Journal of Research in Crime and Delinquency* 21(4): 353-72.

Beyleveld, D. 1980. *A Bibliography of General Deterrence Research.* West-mead, Hampshire: Saxon House.

Biles, D. 1979. "Crime and the Use of Prisons," *Federal Probation* 43 (June): 39-43.

Birch, Roy. 1978. "Corporate Advertising: Why, How and When," *Advertising Quarterly* 57 (5): 5-9.

Blau, P. and O.T. Duncan. 1977. *The American Occupational Structure.* New York: Wiley.

Blum, R. 1984. *Offshore Haven Banks, Trusts, and Companies.* New York: Praeger.

Blumstein, A. and J. Cohen. 1973. "A Theory of the Stability of Punishment," *Journal of Criminal Law and Criminology* 64 (2): 198-207.

Blumstein, A. and S. Moitra. 1979 "An Analysis of the Time Series of the Imprisonment Rate in the United States: A Further Test of the Stability of Punishment Hypothesis," *Journal of Criminal Law and Criminology* 70 (3): 376-390.

Blumstein, A., J. Cohen and D. Nagin. 1977. "The Dynamics of a Homeostatic Punishment Process," *Journal of Criminal Law and Criminology* 67 (3): 317-334.

Blumstein, A., J. Cohen and D. Nagin, eds. 1978. *Deterrence and Incapacitation: Estimating the Effects of Criminal Sanctions on Crime Rates.* Washington, D.C.: National Academy of Sciences.

Boehn, M. 1940-1942 "Der Schoppenstuhl zu Leipzig and der sachsische Inquisitionsprozess im Barockzeitalter" ("The Judiciary of a Leipzig and Saxonia's Inquisitorial Procedure During the Baroque Era"), *Zeitschrift fur die Gesamte Strafrechtswissenachaft* 59 (1940): 371-410 and 620-639; 60 (1941): 155-249; and 61 (1942): 300-403.

Bollen, K.A. 1979. "Political Democracy and the Timing of Development," *American Sociological Review* 44 (August): 572-587.

Bornschier, V. 1978. "Einkommensungleichheit innerhalb von Landern in komparativer Sicht" ("Income Inequality Within Countries in Comparative View"), *Revue suit:in de Sociologie* 4 (1): 3-45.

Bosley, Henry D., 1982. "Responsabilite et Sanctions en Matiere de Criminality des Affairs," *Revue Internationale de Droit Penal* 53: 125-43.

Bowker, L. H. 1981. "Crime and the Use of Prisons in the United States: A Time Series Analysis," *Crime and Delinquency* 27 (April): 206-212.

Box, Steven. 1983. *Crime, Power and Mystification.* London: Tavistock. Braithwaite, J. 1981-82. "The limits of economism in controlling harmful corporate conduct." *Law and Society Review* 16: 481-503.

Braga, Anthony (2017) Arrests, Harm Reduction, and Police Crime Prevention Policy. *Crime and Public Policy.* Volume 16, Issue 2. May. Pages 369-373

Braithwaite, J. 1982a. "Challenging just deserts: Punishing white-collar criminals." *Journal of Criminal Law and Criminology* 73: 723-63.

Braithwaite, J. 1982b "Paradoxes of class bias in criminological research," in *Rethinking Criminology,* ed. H.E. Pepinsky. Beverly Hills: Sage, pp 61-84.

Braithwaite, J. 1984. *Corporate Crime in the Pharmaceutical Industry.* London: Routledge and Kegan Paul.

Braithwaite, J. 1985 *To Punish or Persuade: Enforcement of Coal Mining Safety.* Albany: State University of New York Press.

Braithwaite, J. 1987."Retributivism, Punishment and Privilege," *in Punishment and Privilege,* ed. W.B.Groves and Graeme Newman. New York Harrow and Heston Publishers.

Braithwaite, John and Gilbert Geis. 1982. "On theory and action for corporate crime control," *Crime and Delinquency* 28: 292-314.

Brewer, D., G.E. Beckett, and N. Holt. 1981. "Determinate Sentencing in California: The First Year's Experience," *Journal of Research in Crime and Delinquency* 18 (July): 200-231.

Briloff, A.J. 1972. *Unaccountable Accounting.* New York: Harper and Row

Brogden, Michael. 1982. *The Police: Autonomy and Consent.* London Academic Press.

Bronfenbrenner, M. 1971. *Income Distribution Theory.* Chicago: Aldine and Atherton.

Busey, James L. 1962. *Notes on Costa Rican Democracy.* Boulder: Univ. of Colorado Series in Political Science, no. 2.

Byam, John T. 1982. "The Economic Inefficiency of Corporate Criminal Liability,' *Journal of Criminal Law and Criminology* 73: 582-603.

Cahalan, M. 1979. "Trends in Incarceration in the United States Since 1880" *Crime and Delinquency* 25 (January): 9-41.

Carpzovius, B. 1652. *Practica Nova Imperialis Saxonica* rerum criminalium *in partes III divisa,* Wittenbergae.

Carson, W.G. 1974. "Symbolic and Instrumental Dimensions of Early Factory Legislation," in *Crime, Criminology and Public Policy,* ed. R. Hood. London: Heinemann.

Chambliss, William. 1967. "Types of behavior and the effectiveness of legal sanctions." *Wisconsin Law Review* 3: 703-719.

Changing Work. 1984. *Changing Work: A Magazine About Liberating Work-life.* New Haven, CN.

Christie, Nils. 1968. "Changes in Penal Values," *Scandinavian Studies in Criminology* 2: 161-172.

Christie, Nils. 1974. "Utility and Social Values in Court Decisions in Punishment," in *Crime, Criminology and Public Policy,* ed. R. Hood. New York: Macmillan Publishers, 281-296.

Christie, Nils. 1977. "Conflicts as property," *British Journal of Criminology* 17 (January): 1-19.

Christie, Nils. 1981. *Limits to Pain.* Oxford: Martin Robertson. New York: Oxford University Press.

Clarke, Ronald V. and Graeme R. Newman (2005) Designing out Crime from Products and Systems, *Crime Prevention Studies.* Vol. 17. CA. Lynne Reinner.

Clarke Ronald V. and Graeme R. Newman (2006). *Outsmarting the Terrorists.* Westport. CT.: Praeger.

Clarke, Ronald V. 2016. Criminology and the fundamental attribution error. *The Criminologist.*

Clarke, R. 1979. *The Japanese Company.* New Haven: Yale University Press.

Clifford, William. 1976. *Crime Control in* Japan. Lexington, Mass.: Lexington Books.

Clinard, M.B. 1978. *Cities With Little Crime: The Case of Switzerland.* Cambridge: Cambridge University Press.

Clinard, M. and P. Yeager. 1980. *Corporate Crime.* New York: Free Press.

Coffee, John C. Jr. 1981. "'No Soul to Damn: No Body to Kick' : An Un-scandalized Inquiry Into the Problem of Corporate Punishment," *Michigan Law Review* 79: 386-388.

Coffee, John C. Jr. 1980. "Corporate Crime and Punishment: A Non-Chicago View of the Economics of Criminal Sanctions," *American Criminal Law Review* 17: 419-76.

Cohen, Wilbur. 1980. *Testimony given before the U.S. House of Representatives, Select Committee on Aging,* "Medicare: a fifteen-year perspective." Washington, D.C.: Government Printing Office.

Coser, L.A. 1956. *The Functions of Social Conflict. New* York: The Free Press.

Cranston, R. 1979. *Regulating Business: Law and Consumer Agencies.* London: Macmillan.

Critchley, Thomas A. 1978. A *History of Policing in England and Wales.* London: Constable and Company.

Dahrendorf, R. 1959. *Class and Class Conflict in Industrial Society.* Stanford: Stanford University Press.

Dahrendorf, Ralph. 1979. *Life Chances.* Illinois: The University of Chicago Press.

Deci, Edward L. 1980. *The Psychology of Self-Determination.* Mass.: Lexington Books.

Delatte, Pierre. 1980. "La Question de la Responsibilite Penale des Personnes Morales en Droit Beige," *Revue de Droit Penal et de Criminologic* 60: 191-223.

Dershowitz, Alan M. 1961. "Increasing Community Control Over Corporate Crime: A Problem in the Law of Sanctions," *Yale Law Journal* 71: 280306.

Djilas, M. 1957. *The New Class. An Analysis of the Communist System.* New York: Praeger.

Doleschal, E. 1979. *Median Time Served by Prison Inmates.* Hackensack, N.J.: National Council on Crime and Delinquency, unpublished paper.

Domhoff, William G. 1967. *Who Rules America? New* Jersey: Prentice Hall.

Durkheim, E. 1893/1964. *The Division of Labor in Society.* New York: The Free Press.

Durkheim, E. 1895/1964. *The Rules of Sociological Method.* New York: The Free Press.

Durkheim, E. 1900/1969. "Two Laws of Penal Evolution," *University o) Cincinnati Law Review* 38(1): 32-60.

Elzinga, Kenneth G. and William Breit. 1976. *The Antitrust Penalties: A Study in Law and Economics.* New Haven: Yale U. Press.

Ermann, D. and R. Lundman. 1978. "Deviant acts by complex organizations: deviance and social control at the organizational level of analysis," *Sociological Quarterly* 19: 55-67.

Ermann, D. and R. Lundman, eds. 1982. *Corporate and Governments Deviance: Problems of Organizational Behavior in Contemporary Society.* Second Edition. New York: Oxford University Press.

Falandysz, Lech. 1982. "Victimology in the radical perspective," *in The Victim in International Perspective,* ed. Hans Joachim Schneider. Berlin: De Gruyter, pp. 105-15.

Feagin, Joe R. *1975.Subordinating the Poor: Welfare and American Beliefs.* New Jersey: Prentice Hall.

Federal Bureau of Investigation. *Crime in the United States: Uniform Crime Reports.* Washington, D.C.: U. S. Govt. Printing Office.

Felstiner, William L.P. 1974. "Influences of social organization on dispute processing," *Law and Society Review* 9 (Fall): 63-94.

Fisse, Brent. 1971. "The Use of Publicity as a Criminal Sanction Against Business Corporations," *Melbourne University Law Review* 8: 107-50.

Fisse, Brent. 1973. "Responsibility, Prevention and Corporate Crime," *New Zealand Universities Law Review* 5: 250-279.

Fisse, Brent. 1978. "The Social Policy of Corporate Criminal Responsibility," *Adelaide Law Review* 6: 371-82.

Fisse, Brent. 1980. "Criminal Law and Consumer Protection," in *Consumer Protection Law and Theory,* ed. A. J. Duggan and L. W. Darvall. Sydney: Law Book Company, 182-99.

Fisse, Brent. 1983. "Reconstructing Corporate Criminal Law: Deterrence, Retribution, Fault, and Sanctions," *Southern California Law Review* 56: 1141-1246.

Fisse, Brent and John Braithwaite. *The Impact of Publicity on Corporate Offenders.* Albany: State University of New York Press.

Foucault, Michel. 1977. *Discipline and Punish.* New York: Pantheon.
Foucault, Michel. *1979 .Discipline and Punish.* New York: Vintage.

Fox, Richard. 1982. "Corporate Sanctions: Scope for New Eclecticism," *Malaya Law Review* 24: 26-47.

Frank, Nancy. 1985. *Crimes Against Health and Safety.* New York: Harrow and Heston.

Frankl, Victor. 1959.Man's *Search for Meaning.* Boston: Beacon Press.

Freidson, Eliot. 1970. *Professional Dominance: The Social Structure of Medical Care.* New York: Atherton.

Freidson, Eliot. 1975. *Doctoring Together.* Chicago: University of Chicago Press.

Freilberg, Arie. 1983. "Monetary Penalties Under the Trade Practices Act 1974," *Australian Business Law Review* 11: 4-26.

Freilich, Joshua and Graeme R. Newman. 2018. The New Criminology of Crime Control. *The Annals of the American Academy of Political and Social Science..* September: Sage.

French, Peter. "Publicity and the Control of Corporate Conduct: Hester Prynne's New Image," in *Incorrigible Corporations and Unruly Law,* ed. B. Fisse and P. French, ch. 8.

Galtung, Johan. 1969. "Violence, peace and peace research," *Journal of Peace Research* 6 (July): 167-91.

Garofalo, J. 1979. *Social Structure and Rates of Imprisonment.* Paper presented at the annual meeting of the Academy of Criminal Justice Sciences, Cincinnati, Ohio, March 15, 1979.

Geerken, Michael and Walter Gove. 1975. "Deterrence: some theoretical considerations," *Law and Society Review* 9: 497-513.

Geis, Gilbert. 1967. "White-collar crime: the heavy electrical equipment case of 1961," in *Criminal Behavior Systems: A Typology,* ed. Marshall Clinard and Richard Quinney. New York: Holt, Rinehart and Winston, pp. 139-150.

Geis, Gilbert. 1973. "Deterring corporate crime," in *Corporate Power in America,* ed. Ralph Nader and Mark Green. New York: Grossman, pp. 182-197.

Geraghty, James A. 1979. "Structural Crime and Institutional Rehabilitation: A New Approach to Corporate Sentencing," *Yale Law Journal* 89: 353-75.

Gilbert, D., and J.A. Kahl. 1982. *The American Class Structure.* Homewood, Illinois: The Dorsey Press.

Gillespie, R. W. 1980. "Fines as an Alternative to Incarceration: The German Experience," *Federal Probation* 44 (December): 20-26.

Greenberg, D.F. 1977. "The Dynamics of Oscillatory Punishment Process," *Journal of Criminal Law and Criminology* 68 (4): 643-651.

Greenberg, D.F. 1980. "Penal Sanctions in Poland: A Test of Alternative Models," *Social Problems* 28 (December): 194-204.

Gurinskaya, Anna and Mahesh Nalla. 2018. The expanding boundaries of crime control: Governing security through regulation. *The Annals of the American Academy of Political and Social Science.*. September: Sage.

Gutierrez-Johnson, Ana. 1984. "The Mondragon model of cooperative enterprise: conditions concerning its success and transferability." *Changing Work* 1 (Fall): 35-41.

Hagan, John and Patricia Parker. 1985. "White-collar crime and punishment: the class structure and legal sanctioning of securities violations.' *American Sociological Review* 50: 302-316.

Hale, Richard W. 1908. "The Twenty-Nine Million Dollar Fine," *American Law Review* 41: 904-914.

Hart, H.L.A. 1958. "Legal Responsibility and Excuses," in *Determinism anc Freedom in the Age of Modern Science,* ed. Sidney Hook. New York Collier Books.

Hawkins, K. 1984. *Environment and Enforcement: Regulation and the Social Definition of Pollution.* Oxford: Clarendon.

Hawkins, K. and J.N. Thomas, eds. 1984. *Enforcing Regulation.* Boston Kluwer-Nijhoff.

Hay, D. 1975. "Property, Authority and the Criminal Law," in *Albion's Fatal Tree: Crime* and *Society in Eighteenth Century England,* ed. D. Hay et al. New York: Pantheon Books.

Hayes, Thomas C. 1980. "Complying with EPA Rules," *New York Times:* Dl.

Hawkins, Keith. 1984. *Environment and Enforcement.* Oxford: Clarendon Press.

Heintz, P. 1972. "Structural and Anomic Tensions," in *A Macrosociological Theory of Societal Systems,* ed. P. Heintz, vol. 1. Berne, Switzerland: Huber.

Henk, Thomas and Chris Logan. 1982. *Mondragon: An Economic Analysis.* London/Boston: George Allen and Unwin.

Herlihy, Edward D. and Theodore A. Levine. 1976. "Corporate Crisis: The Overseas Payment Problem," *Law and Policy in International Business* 8: 547-629.

Hindelang, M.J., et al., eds. 1981. *Sourcebook of Criminal Justice Statistics, 1980.* Washington, D.C.: U.S. Government Printing Office.

Hirschi, Travis. 1969. *Causes of Delinquency.* Berkeley: University of California Press.

Hirst, P.Q. 1975. "Marx and Engels on Law, Crime, and Morality," in *Critical Criminology,* ed. I. Taylor et al. London: Routledge and Kegan Paul.

Hopkins, Andrew. 1978. *The Impact of Prosecutions Under the Trade Practices Act.* Canberra: Australian Institute of Criminology.

Hough, Mike, and Pat Mayhew. 1985. "Taking Account of Crime: Key Findings of the 1984 British Crime Survey." *Home Office Research Studies.* (July) Report No. 85.

Hutt, P. 1973. "The philosophy of regulation under the federal Food, Drug and Cosmetic Act." *Food, Drug and Cosmetic Law Journal* 28: 177.

Ignatieff, M. 1978. A *Just Measure of Pain: The Penitentiary in the Industrial Revolution, 1750-1850.* New York: Pantheon Books.

Immarigeon, Russell. 1984. "Victim-offender reconciliation programs and the criminal justice system: confusion and challenge." *VORP Network News* 3 (Fall): 4, 7-9.

Inciardi, James. 1984.Criminal *Justice. New* York: Academic Press.

Jevons, William S. 1871. *The Theory of Political Economy.* New York: MacMillan.

James, W. 1910 "The Moral Equivalent of War," *McClures Magazine,* August 1910. Reprinted in James, 1971 *The Essential Writings.* New York: Harper, pp. 349-61.

Jankovic, I. 1977. "Labor Market and Imprisonment," *Crime and Social Justice* 8 (Fall-Winter): 17-31.

Kaiser, G. 1976. *Criminologic,* 3rd edition. Heidelberg, FRG: C. F. Muller.

Katz, Jack. 1979. "Legality and equality: plea bargaining in the prosecution of white-collar and common crimes." *Law and Society Review* 13: 431-459.

Katzmann, Robert A. 1980. "Judicial Intervention and Organization Theory: Changing Bureaucratic Behavior and Policy," *Yale Law Journal* 98: 513-37.

Kipnis, D. 1972. "Does Power Corrupt?" *Journal of Personality and Social Psychology* 24 (1): 33-41.

Knightley, P., H. Evans, H. Potter and E. Wallace. 1979. *Suffer the Children: the Story of Thalidomide.* New York: Viking.

Kolko, Gabriel. 1962. *Wealth and Power in America: An Analysis of Social Class and Income Distribution.* New York: Praeger.

Kornhauser, R.R. 1978. *Social Sources of Delinquency: An Appraisal of Analytic Models.* Chicago: University of Chicago Press.

Kramer, Ronald C. 1982. "From 'habitual offenders' to 'career criminals': the historical development of criminal categories," Law and Human *Behavior* 6 (3/4): 273-93.

Kramer, Ronald C. 1984. "Corporate Criminality: The Development of an Idea," *in Corporations as Criminals,* ed. Ellen Hochstedler. Beverly Hills: Sage, pp. 13-37.

Kriesberg, Simeon M. 1976. "Decision Making Models and the Control of Corporate Crime," *Yale Law Journal* 85: 1091-1129.

Krisberg, Barry. 1975. *Crime and Privilege.* New Jersey: Prentice Hall.

Lanza-Kaduce, Lonn. 1980. "Deviance among professionals: the case of unnecessary surgery." *Deviant Behavior* 1: 333-359.

Lemert, E. 1951. *Social Pathology.* New York: McGraw-Hill.

Levin, Marjorie J. 1984. "Corporate Probation Conditions: Judicial Creativity or Abuse of Discretion?" *Fordham Law Review* 52: 637-662.

Lipton, D., R. Martinson and J. Wilks. 1975. *The Effectiveness of Correctional Treatment: A Survey of Treatment Evaluation Studies.* New York: Praeger.

Lopez-Rey, M. 1980. "General Overview of Capital Punishment as a Legal Sanction," *Federal Probation* 44 (March): 18-23.

Luhmann, N. 1975. *Macht* (Power). Stuttgart, FRG: Enke.

Lynch, M. and W. B. Groves. 1986. *A Primer in Radical Criminology.* New York: Harrow and Heston.

Martinson, Robert. 1974. "What works?: questions and answers about prison reform," *The Public Interest* 35: 22-54.

Marx, K. 1967. *Capital.* New York: International.

Marx, K. 1970a. *A Contribution to the Critique of Political Economy.* New York: International.

Marx. K. 1970b. *Critique of the Gotha Programme.* New York: International.

Maslow, Abraham. 1982. *The Farther Reaches of* Human *Nature. New* York: Penguin Books.

Matza, David. 1964. *Delinquency and Drift.* New York: John Wiley and Sons.

Maxfield, Michael G. and Ronald V. Clarke (Eds.) (2004). Understanding and Preventing Car Theft, *Crime. Prevention Studies.* Vol. 18. CA. Lynne Reinner.

McAdams, John B. 1977. "The Appropriate Sanctions for Corporate Criminal Liability: An Eclectic Alternative," *Cincinnati Law Review* 46: 9891000.

McCloy, John J. 1976. *The Great Oil Spill: The Inside Report.* New York:. Chelsea House Publishers.

Melossi, D. and M. Pavarini. 1979. *Carcere e fabbrica. Alle origini del sistema penitenziario (XVI-XIX secolo),* (Prison and Factory. The Origins of the System of Corrections, 16th to 19th centuries), 2nd edition. Bologna, Italy: Il Mulino.

Melossi, Dario, and Massimo Pavarini. 1981. *The Prison and the Factory: Origins of the Penitentiary System.* Trans. by Glynis Cousin. Totowa, N.J.: Barnes and Noble.

Mendeloff, J. 1979. *Regulating Safety: An Economic and Political Analysis of Occupational Safety and Health Policy.* Cambridge, Mass.: MIT Press.

Michalowski, Raymond. 1985.*Order, Law, and Crime.* New York: Random House.

Miller, S. M. and P. Roby. 1970. *The Future of Inequality.* New York: Basic Books.

Mills, C.W. 1963. in *Power, Politics, and People,* ed. I. Horowitz. London: Oxford University Press .

Mitchell, Jerry and Janet Cromwell. 1982. "Medicaid participation by physicians in private practice," *American Journal of Psychiatry* 139: 810-813.

Montero, Jorge A. 1983. "Costa Rica," in *International Handbook of Contemporary Developments in Criminology: General Issues and the Americas,* ed. Elmer Johnson. Westport, Conn.: Greenwood Press, pp. 233-49.

Montesquieu, C.L. 1948/1977. *The Spirit of Laws,* ed. D. W. Carrithers. Berkeley, California: University of California Press.

Morris, N. 1974. *The Future of Imprisonment.* Chicago: University of Chicago Press.

Mulder, M. 1960. "The Power Variable in Communication Experiments," Human *Relations* 13: 241-257.

Murphy, J. 1979. *Retribution, Justice and Therapy.* Boston: D. Reidel.

Nader, Laura, and Philip Parnell. 1983. "Comparative Law and Enforcement: Preliterate Societies," *in Encyclopedia of Criminal Justice,* ed. Sanford Kadish. New York: Macmillan, pp. 200-7.

Nagel, G. W. 1977. "On Behalf of a Moratorium on Prison Construction," *Crime and Delinquency* 23 (April): 154-172.

Nettler, G. 1974. *Explaining Crime.* New York: MacMillan.

Newman, Graeme. 1983. *Just and Painful: A Case for the Corporal Punishment of Criminals.* New York: Macmillan.

Newman, Graeme. 1985. *The Punishment Response.* New York: Harrow and Heston.

Newman, Graeme R. (2008). *The Punishment Response* 2nd edition with new introduction. NJ.: Transaction Press.

Newman, G.R., and E. Vetere. 1978. *World Crime: A Comparative Analysis,* State University of New York: unpublished manuscript.

Nie, N.H., et al. 1975. *SPSS (Statistical Package for the Social Sciences),* 2nd edition. New York: McGraw-Hill.

Nisbet, R. A. 1966. *The Sociological Tradition.* New York: Basic Books. Oakeshott, Robert. 1978. *The Case for Workers' Co-ops.* London/Boston: Routledge and Kegan Paul.

Office of Inspector General, U.S. Department of Health and Human Services. 1983. *New Efforts to Combat Medicare and Medicaid Fraud and Abuse.* Washington, D.C.: Government Printing Office.

Olins, Wally. 1978. *The Corporate Personality: An Inquiry into the Nature of Corporate Identity.* New York: Mayflower Books.

Otley, Bruce. 1982. "Criminal Liability for Defective Products: New Problems in Corporate Responsibility and Sanctioning," *Revue Internationale de Droit Penal* 53: 145-170.

Parsons, Talcott. 1951. *The Social System.* New York: Free Press.

Pepinsky, Harold E. 1980. *Crime Control Strategies.* New York: Oxford University Press.

Pepinsky, Harold E., and Paul Jesilow. 1982. "A season of disenchantment: trends in Chinese justice reconsidered,"

International Journal of the Sociology of Law 10 (August): 277-285.

Pepinsky, Harold E., and Paul Jesilow. 1985. *Myths That Cause Crime.* (2nd ann. edn.) Cabin John, Md.: Seven Locks Press.

Pepinsky, Harold E., and Paul Jesilow. 1986. "Justice as information sharing," in *The Decentralization of Social Control,* ed. John Lowman, Robert J. Menzies and T.S. Palys. Aldershot, U.K.: Gower Publishing Co.

Pfohl, S.J. 1985. *Images of Deviance and Social Control. N. Y.:* McGraw-Hill.

Platek, Monika. 1985. "The contemporary situation in Polish prisons." Colloquium given at Criminal Justice Consortium, Indiana University, Bloomington, September 20.

Platt, Anthony. 1982. "Crime and Punishment in the United States: Immediate and Long-Term Reforms from a Marxist Perspective," *Crime and Social Justice* 18: 38-45.

Pontell, H. 1978 "Deterrence: Theory versus practice," *Criminology* 16: 330.

Pontell, Henry N. 1982. "System capacity and criminal justice: theoretical and substantive considerations," in *Rethinking Criminology,* ed. Harold E. Pepinsky. Beverly Hills: Sage Publications, pp. 131-143.

Pontell, Henry N. 1984. *A Capacity to Punish: The Ecology of Crime and Punishment.* Bloomington: Indiana University Press.

Pontell, Henry N., Paul D. Jesilow, and Gilbert Geis. 1984. "Practitioner fraud and abuse in medical benefit programs: government regulation and professional white-collar crime," *Law and Policy* 6 (October): 405-424.

Posner, Richard. 1977. *Economic Analysis of Law* 2nd ed. Boston: Little, Brown.

Posner, Richard. 1980. "Optimal Sentences for White-Collar Criminals," *American Criminal Law Review* 17: 409-418.

President's Commission on Law Enforcement and Administration of Justice. 1967. *The Challenge of Crime in a Free Society.* Washington, D.C.: Government Printing Office.

Quinney, Richard. 1977. *Class, State, and Crime.* New York: David McKay.

Quinney, Richard. 1974. Critique of the Legal Order., Boston: Little Brown.

Radig, James W. 1985. "Corporate Contributions to Charity as a Condition of Probation under the Federal Probation *Act,*" *The Journal of Corporation Law* 9: 241-269.

Ranulf, Svend. 1964. *Moral Indignation and Middle Class Psychology: A Sociological Study.* New York: Schocken Books.

Reiman, J. 1984. *The Rich Get Richer and the Poor Get Prison* 2nd edition. New York: John Wiley and Sons.

Reynolds, M. and E. Smolensky. 1977. *Public Expenditures, Taxes, and the Distribution of Income.* New York: Academic Press.

Root, Howard and Stephen Saltarelli (2026) *Cardiac Arrest: Five Heart-Stopping Years as a CEO On the Feds' Hit-List.* Kindle. Bookbaby

Rosoff, Steven. 1984. *Physicians as Criminal Defendants: Doctor Williams, Mr. Williams, and the Ambivalence Hypothesis.* Unpublished M.A. thesis. Program in Social Ecology, University of California, Irvine.

Ross, E. A. 1901/1959. *Social Control and the Foundatons of Sociology,* ed. E. F. Borgatta and H. J. Meyer. Boston: Beacon Press.

Ross, Edward. 1907. "The criminaloid," *The Atlantic Monthly* 99: 44-50.

Round, David. 1985. "Does the Punishment Fit the Crime? An Analysis of Antitrust Penalties in Australia." Paper presented at Trade Practices Workshop, Center for Commercial Law and Applied Legal Research, June, 44: 28-30.

Rusche, G. 1933. "Arbeitsmarkt and Strafvollzug: Gedanken zur Soziologie der Strafjustiz" ("The Labor Market and Corrections: On the Sociology of Criminal Justice"), *Zeitschrift fur Sozialforschung* 2: 63-78.

Rusche, G., and 0. Kirchheimer. 1939. *Punishment and Social Structure.* New York: Columbia University Press.

Sartre, J. P. 1976. "Existentialism," in *Existentialism 2,* ed. W. Spanos. New York: Thomas Y. Crowell Co.

Sartre, J. P. 1978. *Being and Nothingness.* N.Y.: Pocket Books.

Schell, Orville. 1984. "Crime and capitalism in China," *CoEvolution Quarterly* 42 (Summer): 30-37.

Schneider, H. D. 1978. *Sozialpsychologie der Machtbeziehungen* (Social Psychology of Power Relationships). Stuttgart, FRFG: Enke.

Schrag, P. G. 1971. "On Her Majesty's secret service: protecting the consumer in New York city," *Yale Law Journal* 80: 1529-1603.

Schrager, L.S. and J.F. Short Jr. 1978. "Toward a sociology of organizational *crime,"* *Social Problems* 25: 407-19.

Screvens, Raymond. 1980. "Les Sanctions Applicables aux Personnes Morales dans les Etats des Communautes Europeenes," *Revue de Droit Penale et de Criminologie* 60: 163-190.

Selke, William L. and Harold E. Pepinsky. 1982. "Police reporting in Indianapolis, 1948-78," Law and Human *Behavior* 6 (3/4): 327-42.

Shelley, L. I. 1981. *Crime and Modernization.* Carbondale: Southern Illinois University Press.

Shover, N., D.A. Clelland and J. Lynxwiler. 1983. *Developing a Regulatory Bureaucracy: The Office of Surface Mining Reclamation and Enforcement.* Washington, D.C.: National Institute of Justice.

Simmel, G. 1950. *The Sociology of Georg Simmel.* New York: *Free Press.*

Simmel, G. 1955. *Conflict and the Web of Group Affiliations.* New York: Free Press.

Simmel, G. 1959. *Essays in Sociology, Philosophy and Aesthetics.* New York: Harper and Row.

Singer, R.G. 1979. *Just Desert: Sentencing Based on Equality and Desert.* Cambridge, Mass.: Ballinger.

Smith, A. 1970. *Adam Smith's Moral and Political Philosophy.* ed. H. Schneider. New York: Harper.

Smith. G. 1968. "Determinism, Freedom and Responsibility," *Issues in Criminology* 3, 2.

Solomon, Lewis D. and Nancy Stein Nowak. 1980. "Managerial Restructuring: Prospects for a New Regulatory Tool," *Notre Dame Lawyer* 56: 120-140.

Solzhenitsyn, Alexander. 1974. *The Gulag Archipelago. New* York: Harper and Row.

Sorokin, P. A. 1937. *Social and Cultural Dynamics, vol. 2: Fluctuation of Systems of Truth, Ethics, and Law.* New York: Bedminster Press.

Stanbury, W. T. 1976. "Penalties and Remedies Under the Combines Investigation Act 1889-1976," *Osgoode Hall Law* Journal 14: 571-631.

Steinert, H., and H. Treiber. 1978. "Versuch die These von der strafrechtlichen Ausrottungspolitik im Spatmittelalter causzurotten"(Attempt to Exterminate the Theory of Crime Extermination Policy During the Late Middle-Ages"), *Kriminologiuches Journal* 10(2): 81-106.

Stone, C. 1975. *Where the Law Ends: The Social Control of Corporate Behavior.* New York: Harper and Row.

Stone, Christopher D. 1977. "A Slap on the Wrist for the Kepone Mob," *Business and Society Review* 22: 4-11.

Sutherland, Edwin H. 1949. *White Collar Crime.* New York: Dryden. Sutherland, Edwin H. 1934. *Principles of Criminology.* Chicago: J.B. Lippincott Co.

Sutherland, Edwin H. 1983. *White Collar Crime: The Uncut Version.* New Haven: Yale University Press.

Sutherland, Edwin H. 1940. "White-collar criminality," *American Sociological Review* 5 (February): 1-12.

Sutton, A. and R. Wild. 1978. "Corporate crime and social structure," in *Two Faces of Deviance: Crimes of the Powerless and Powerful* ed. P.R. Wilson and J. Braithwaite. Brisbane: University of Queensland Press, pp.177-198.

Sutton, A. and R. Wild. 1979. "Companies, the law and the professions," in *Legislation and Society in Australia,* ed. R. Tomasic. Sydney: Allen and Unwin, 200-212.

Taylor, I. 1980. "The Law and Order Issue in the British General Election and the Canadian Federal Election of 1979: Crime,

Populism, and the State," *Canadian Journal of Sociology* 5(3): 285-310.

Taylor, I., P. Walton and J. Young. 1973. *The New Criminology.* New York: Harper and Row.

Tiedemann, K. 1980. "Antitrust Law and Criminal Law Policy in Western Europe," in *Economic Crime in Europe,* ed. L. H. Leigh. London: MacMillan, pp. 39-56.

Tifft, Larry L. 1985. "Reflections on capital punishment and the campaign against crime in China," *Justice Quarterly* 2 (March): 127-137.

Tifft, Larry L. and Dennis Sullivan. 1980. *The Struggle to Be Human: Crime, Criminology, and Anarchism.* Over the Water, Sanday, Orkney, U.K.: Cienfuegos Press.

Tittle, C.R., W.J. Villemez and D.A. Smith. 1978. "The Myth of Social *Class* and Criminality: An Empirical Assessment of Empirical Evidence," *American Sociological Review* 43 (October): 643-656.

Turk, Austin. 1969. *Criminality and Legal Order.* Chicago: Rand McNally.

Udy, S. 1965. "Dynamic Inferences from Static Data," *American Journal of Sociology* 70: 625-627.

United States National Commission on Reform of Federal Criminal Laws. 1970. *Study Draft.* Washington, D. C.: United States Government Printing Office.

van den Haag, Ernest. 1975. *Punishing Criminals: Concerning a Very Old and Painful Question.* New York: Basic Books.

van den Haag, Ernest. 1982. "Could successful rehabilitation retard the crime *rate?" Journal of Criminal Law and Criminology* 73 (Fall): 10221035.

van den Haag, Ernest. 1983. "The effects of criminal punishment: is selective incapacitation a good idea?" Paper presented at the American Society of Criminology Meeting, Denver.

van den Haag, Ernest 1987. "On Sentencing," *in Punishment and Privilege,* ed. W.B. Groves and Graeme Newman. New York: Harrow and Heston.

van Dine, S., J.P. Conrad, and S. Dinitz. 1979. *Restraining the Wicked.* Lexington, Mass.: Lexington Books.

van Fossen, Beth. 1979. *The Structure of Social Inequality.* New York: Little, Brown and Co.

Veljanovski, Cento G. 1984 "The Economics of Regulatory Enforcement," in *Enforcing Regulation,* ed. Keith Hawkins and John M. Thomas. Boston: Kluwer, Ch. 8.

Vold, G.B. and T.J. Bernard. 1986. *Theoretical Criminology.* New York: Oxford.

von Hirsch, A. 1976. *Doing Justice: The Choice of Punishments.* New York: Hill and Wang.

Waller, Irvin, and Janet Chan. 1974. "Prison use: a Canadian and international comparison," *Criminal Law Quarterly* 17 (December): 47-71.

Wallster, E., et al. 1973. "New Directions in Equity Research," *Journal of*

Weber, Max. 1925/1954. *Max Weber on Law in Economy and Society*, ed. M. Rheinstein. New York: Simon and Schuster.

Weber, Max. 1977. *From Max Weber,* ed. H. Gerth and C. Wright Mills. London: Oxford University Press.

Weede, E. 1981. "Militar, Multis and Wirtschaft" ("Military, MNC and Economy"), *Revue suisse de sociologic 7(1):* 113-127.

West, D.J. and D. P. Farrington. 1977. *The Delinquent Way of Life.* London: Heinemann.

Wilkins, L. T. 1965. *Social Deviance.* Englewood Cliffs, N. J.: Prentice-Hall. Wilkins, L. T. 1974. "Directions for Corrections," *Proceedings of the American Philosophical Society* 118: 235-247.

Wilkins, L. T. 1976. "Equity and Republican Justice," *Annals of the American Academy of Political and Social Science* 423: 152-161.

Wilkins, L. T. 1984. *Consumerist Criminology.* London: Heinemann. Totowa, N.J.: Barnes and Noble.

Wilson, James Q. 1975. *Thinking About Crime.* New York: Basic Books.

Wilson, J. Q. and R. J. Herrenstein. 1985. *Crime and Human Nature. N.Y.:* Simon and Schuster.

Wolff, Jacqueline. 1979. "Voluntary Disclosure Programs," *Fordham Law Review* 47: 1057-1082.

Wolfgang, M. 1973. "Crime in a birth cohort," *Proceedings of the American Philosophical Society* 117; 404.

Wolfgang, M. 1980. National Survey of Crime Severity. Center for Studies in Criminology and Criminal Law, University of Pennsylvania, April, Unpublished manuscript.

Yashihara, Nancy. 1981. "$1 Billion Spent on Identity: Companies Push Image of Selves, Not Products," *Los Angeles Times May* 10, pt.6: 1.

Yeager, M. G. 1979. "Unemployment and Imprisonment," *Journal of Criminal Law and Criminology* 70(4): 586-588.

Yoder, Stephen A. 1978 "Criminal Sanctions for Corporate Illegality," *Journal of Criminal Law and Criminology* 69: 40-58.

Ziegler, Jean. 1979. *Switzerland: The Awful Truth.* Trans Rosemary Steed Middleton. New York: Harper and Row.

Zimring, Franklin E. and Gordon J. Hawkins. 1973. *Deterrence: The Legal Threat in Crime Control.* Chicago: University of Chicago Press.

Zinn, Howard. 1980. *A People's History of the United States.* New York: Harper Colophon.